ALSO BY ERIK PETTERSEN

Semper Fi: The Psalms of Robert Alexander

Limericks for Polite Company

LEAP OF FAITH

*A Trans-Atlantic Wartime
Love Story*

By
Erik Pettersen

All rights reserved. No part of this book shall be reproduced or transmitted in any form or by any means, electronic, mechanical, magnetic, photographic including photocopying, recording or by any information storage and retrieval system, without prior written permission of the publisher. No patent liability is assumed with respect to the use of the information contained herein. Although every precaution has been taken in the preparation of this book, the publisher and author assume no responsibility for errors or omissions. Neither is any liability assumed for damages resulting from the use of the information contained herein.

Copyright © 2012 by Erik Pettersen

ISBN 978-0-7414-7822-1 Paperback
ISBN 978-0-7414-7823-8 Hardcover
ISBN 978-0-7414-7829-0 eBook

Printed in the United States of America

Published August 2012

INFINITY PUBLISHING
1094 New DeHaven Street, Suite 100
West Conshohocken, PA 19428-2713
Toll-free (877) BUY BOOK
Local Phone (610) 941-9999
Fax (610) 941-9959
Info@buybooksontheweb.com
www.buybooksontheweb.com

This book is dedicated to the loving memory of my mother. It fulfills a longstanding promise I made to myself -- to pass on her story for future generations.

Contents

Foreword vii
Introduction ix
1. The Beginning 1
2. A Family of Clergy 5
3. Ingrid Remembers: My Early Years 13
4. Whence the Pettersens 31
5. Stefanus and Lydia 37
6. "Iron Brain" 45
7. Ingrid Remembers: Growing Up 49
8. American Bride 59
9. A Swede in America 83
10. Love and War 87
11. First Christmas in America 95
12. A New Year 101
13. A New Life 117
14. "In Sickness and in Health" 123
15. Alice's First Christmas 127
16. The War Years 131
17. Peace at Last 141
18. Early Memories 147
Epilogue 151
Acknowledgments 153
Notes 157

Foreword

I have many cherished memories of my father's mother Ingrid, my Farmor. I consider myself blessed to have known and spent so much time with her as a granddaughter. I remember her as vibrant and talented, with the biggest heart in the world and giving the best hugs. I remember swims in the lake by her house, trips to the Catskill Game Farm, baking cookies and apple cake, and playing and singing duets with her at the piano. Throughout these visits with Farmor I remember the stories, especially the ones about her life growing up as the youngest daughter of a pastor in rural Sweden and her journey to America to marry my Farfar.

As I grew older, I recognized that each of my Farmor's memories knit together created a wonderful narrative. This idea was reaffirmed after I received a translation of one of her journals when I was a young adult. I am so thankful that my father decided to write this book. It beautifully weaves my Farmor's own words with the supporting facts and history surrounding her life. He fills many gaps in the stories I have known since childhood, including her incredible voyage across the Atlantic. His book is also full of things I learned for the very first time. For those readers who were not fortunate to know and love my Farmor, the book is a timeless story of love and one woman's "leap of faith."

Kristen Pettersen Morgan
Stafford, Virginia

Introduction

I have led a very blessed life. As a first generation American, I was nurtured by two unique and loving parents whose courtship and marriage made the front page in the New York newspapers in June 1941. Theirs remains an oft-told story by succeeding generations of their respective families, as I am reminded every time I visit with my Scandinavian relatives. Consider these improbable circumstances:

- Before he emigrated from Norway to the United States in 1937, my father had seen my mother only twice;
- Nearly three years later, he wrote her a letter asking for her hand in marriage, and she accepted in a telegram;
- When she left Sweden in late May 1941, the war in Europe had already broken out, Norway had been occupied by the Germans, and the Battle of the Denmark Strait was fought not far from her ship's transit route, only three days after it had left port;
- Just seventeen days after she arrived in New York, my mother and my father were married.

Several of my relatives assisted enthusiastically by providing documents and pictures when they learned of my attempt to put this story to paper. But my primary source has been my mother. One year, I believe some time in the 1980s, she asked what I would like for Christmas. Aware that she had done something similar for one of my sisters, I responded that I would love to have her give me a recording of remembrances from her childhood and youth. She fulfilled my wish, and to this day I have retained that cassette of her beautiful voice. My son Matthew has made copies on CDs. Portions of the transcript have been included in Chapters 3, 7, 8 and 9.

After my mother's passing in 1995, I recovered two leather diaries from my parents' attic. In them, my mother had recorded events from the first eighteen months of her married life. They were translated from Swedish into English for me by my late cousin, Stig Törnqvist, whom I always suspected was my mother's favorite nephew. Excerpts from her diaries are included in Chapters 10 through 15.

My father's interest in his family's genealogy played an important role in this story. His dogged research into learning about both sides of my family was invaluable in putting together Chapters 2, 4, 5 and 6. But for his diligence, this story never would have happened.

CHAPTER 1

The Beginning

Violence is the last resort of the foolish.
(Swedish proverb)

Throughout my life, when I have told friends and acquaintances about my parents, I invariably mention that my father came to the United States from Norway and that my mother arrived several years later from Sweden. A frequent response is one of surprise, almost as though a Hatfield had married a McCoy, for stories of rivalry between the two countries are common. A broader historical and geographic perspective is therefore probably in order.

Although the history of the Scandinavian countries goes back thousands of years, for the purposes of my narrative I will just go back as far as the year 1319, when King Haakon V of Norway died, leaving no male heirs. The king's daughter Ingeborg married a Swedish prince, whose son Magnus Eriksson[1] inherited both kingdoms. When Magnus later abdicated his throne in 1343, his son, Haakon VI became king of Norway. In 1363, Haakon VI married Princess Margaret of Denmark, who was only ten years old at the time. In 1397, the now Queen Margaret played a pivotal role in uniting Norway, Denmark and Sweden in what became known as the Kalmar Union. Although each country retained some degree of autonomy, Denmark was the dominant power. The countries shared a single monarch, and the aggregate population was only about three million people. Norway's power was weakened during this period by the loss of approximately one third of its population during the bubonic plague (Black Death) pandemic of 1349–1351. The Kalmar Union remained in tact for 126 years, until Sweden's secession in 1523.

In the 1530s the Protestant Reformation reached Norway, and the Norwegians followed the Danes in accepting Lutheran doctrines. In 1624, after the town of Oslo was destroyed by a major fire, the Danish king Christian rebuilt it and immodestly renamed it Christiania, after himself. It was to retain that name for the next three hundred years.

In 1813, Swedish forces invaded Denmark, and, in January 1814, forced the surrender of Norway to Sweden. Crown Prince Christian Frederick led a group of Norwegians who rebelled against the annexation by Sweden. He called an assembly which, on May 17, 1814, drew up a constitution, and he was elected king. To this day May 17 is still celebrated as the day of the new democratic constitution of independent Norway.

However, the Swedes invaded Norway just two months later, forcing Christian Frederick to step down and the Norwegians to accept the Swedish king. But in a display of magnanimity he agreed to honor the newly drafted Norwegian constitution and allowed Norway a fair degree of autonomy, including electing its own parliament, the Storting.

The union between the two countries was peacefully dissolved on October 26, 1905 when, after several years of political unrest, Sweden recognized

Norwegian independence. In a referendum the following month, the Norwegians voted for a constitutional monarchy. The Storting offered the crown to Prince Carl of Denmark, who accepted. On November 18 he ascended the throne and assumed the Norwegian name of Haakon VII, an act that endeared him to his newly adopted subjects.

Timeline

1319 – King Haakon VI of Norway dies. His son, Magnus Eriksson becomes hereditary ruler of both Norway and Sweden.

1343 – Magnus abdicates; his son, Haakon VI, becomes king of Norway.

1349-51 – Black Death (bubonic plague) pandemic kills 1/3 of population.

1363 – Haakon VI marries 10-year-old Princess Margaret of Denmark.

1397 – Queen Margaret plays key role in uniting Denmark, Norway and Sweden in the Kalmar Union, with Denmark the dominant power.

1523 – Sweden secedes from the Kalmar Union.

1530s – Protestant Reformation reaches Norway.

1624 – Oslo is destroyed by fire. Danish King Christian rebuilds it and renames the city Christiania after himself.

1813 – Sweden invades Denmark.

1814 – Denmark surrenders Norway to Sweden in January;
 -- Norway draws up and adopts its own constitution on May 17 under leadership of Crown Prince Christian Frederick
 -- Sweden invades Norway in July, forcing Christian Frederick to step down but honoring Norway's newly drafted constitution.

1905 – Union between Norway and Sweden dissolved peacefully on October 26; Norway becomes constitutional monarchy. Crown is offered to Prince Carl of Denmark, who accepts and adopts Norwegian name of Haakon VII.

Chapter 2

A Family of Clergy

But you will be called the priests of the Lord...
Isaiah 61:6

Before the time of the Revolutionary War in America, there lived in the town of Sillerud, Sweden a man by the name of Nils Torsten, who had two sons, Hans and Daniel. In keeping with Swedish custom, their surnames became Nilsson, literally sons of Nils. In 1756, Hans' wife gave birth to their first son, whom they named Nils, in honor of his father. With the others of his generation, Nils adopted the surname Sillén,[2] derived from Sillerud, the town from which his family traced their ancestry. Nine years later, in 1765, Hans' wife gave birth to a second son, whom they named Daniel Hansson Sillén, in honor of his brother. Family records show that the elder Daniel fathered just one son, born in 1788, and that he, too, honored his father by naming him Nils, but differentiated him from his older cousin by adding the middle name Jakob.

Both Nils Sillén and Nils Jakob Sillén became ordained Lutheran ministers, a calling that was to be perpetuated in future generations, including:

- Nils Sillén's three sons, Bengt Johan (born in 1787), Nils Christoffer (1789) and Olof (1794);
- Daniel Hansson Sillén's son Daniel (born in 1793);

- Daniel Sillén's only son, Gustaf Daniel (born in 1832), and his grandson Carl Theofil Ekelund, one of eight children born to his daughter Karolina;
- Three of Gustaf Daniel's four sons: twins Gustav Petrus and Josef Daniel, born in 1869, and Jakob Emanuel (1872); and
- Josef Daniel's two sons who reached adulthood, Gösta (born in 1899) and Erik (1904). His two elder daughters, Anna and Greta, married two brothers, Carl and Bertil Törnqvist, respectively, who were, as you might guess, both ministers. Anna and Carl's first child, Sven (born in 1925), also became a minister.

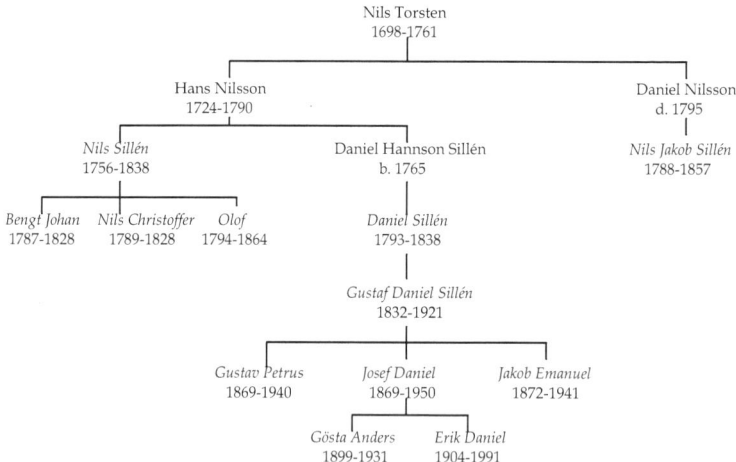

So the Sillén family was replete with clergy, fourteen in all, through six generations. In the simplified family tree above, the clergy are indicated by italics. Biographies of the twelve bearing the Sillén surname are included in a book by my relative Alf Brorson: *Sillénska Anfäder – tolv präster i Värmland och på Dal (Sillén Family Ancestors – Twelve Priests in Värmland and Dal).*

****

My story begins with my great-grandfather, whom my Swedish relatives would identify as my *morfarfar*, or mother's father's father.

Gustaf Daniel Sillén was born on July 19, 1832, to Rev. Daniel and Britte-Louise Sillén in Värmland's capital city of Karlstad, where his father was serving as a pastor. After attending local schools, he enrolled in 1850 at the university in Uppsala, earning a bachelor of medicine degree in 1852, followed by degrees in both theoretical and practical theology in 1860. On September 2 of that year, he was ordained at the castle chapel in Stockholm. In 1867, after serving as both a pastor and teacher in several other parishes, he became the pastor in Gesäter, a rustic farming community in the district of Dalsland, about 125 kilometers north of the city of Göteborg (Gothenburg) and 140 Kilometers south of Christiania (now Oslo). That same year he married Christina Maria Kindberg, from the small town of Hvena in southeastern Sweden, where her father Johan Peter Kindberg was a freeholder.

Gustaf was to serve in Gesäter for thirteen years, until 1880. During his tenure there, Christina bore him eight children, four sons and four daughters. The eldest, Marie Louise, was born in 1868, and the youngest, Hilda Kristina, in 1876. So the age span of this brood was less than nine years! All were born in the parish parsonage known as Prästbo. Christina's second pregnancy resulted in the birth of twin boys on April 8, 1869. They were christened Gustaf Petrus and Josef Daniel. Each went by the name inherited from their father, Gustaf and Daniel, respectively, and both were to follow in their father's footsteps.

The Scandinavian peninsula, highlighting the location of Värmland and Dalsland. Approx. scale: 1" = 160 miles

In the fall of 1880, at the age of eleven, the twins left home and were enrolled in a secondary school in the university town of Uppsala in eastern Sweden, where their Aunt Maria lived. After graduation in 1888, they both enrolled in a theology curriculum at the university. Upon successfully completing all of the requirements, Daniel was ordained into the Lutheran ministry in the Karlstad Cathedral on June 23, 1896. Gustaf was ordained seven months later.

Värmland and Dalsland

Following his ordination, Daniel had a series of short-term assignments in the towns of Torp, Åmål and Nordmark. Then, in the spring of 1897, he became the pastor of the church in Gesäter. He moved into the parsonage where he and his twin brother had been born twenty-eight years earlier, when their father had been the pastor there. A little more than a year later, on May 26, 1898, he married Anna Elisabeth (Alice) Norblad, who was seven years his junior. Alice was born on July 11, 1876 in the little town of Ransäter in central Värmland, the first of two daughters of Anders and Christina Norblad. Anders was a civil engineer, as well as a college director, and Christina was a deaconess.

Perhaps unbeknownst to them at the time, Daniel and Alice actually shared some common ancestry, going back to an Austrian immigrant by the name of Christoffer Geijer, who came to Sweden in 1620 and subsequently married Dorothea Giliusdotter de Besche. This connection is depicted in my father's hand-drawn chart on the following page.

Daniel and Alice had six children, all born in the small parsonage, or Prästbo, in Gesäter. Their first child, Gustaf Anders, nicknamed Gösta, was born on April 14, 1899. Throughout their youth, his younger siblings enjoyed teasing him that he was from another century.

The following year, on November 30, Alice bore a second son, whom they named Ivar Daniel, but he lived less than four months. On May 10, 1902, she gave birth to their first daughter, whom they named Anna. On August 14, 1904, she delivered their third son, whom they christened Erik Daniel. Four years later, on

September 8, 1908, their second daughter, Greta Maria was born. More than seven years elapsed before Alice delivered her sixth and youngest child, another daughter, on November 27, 1915. They named her Ingrid Christina Sillén.

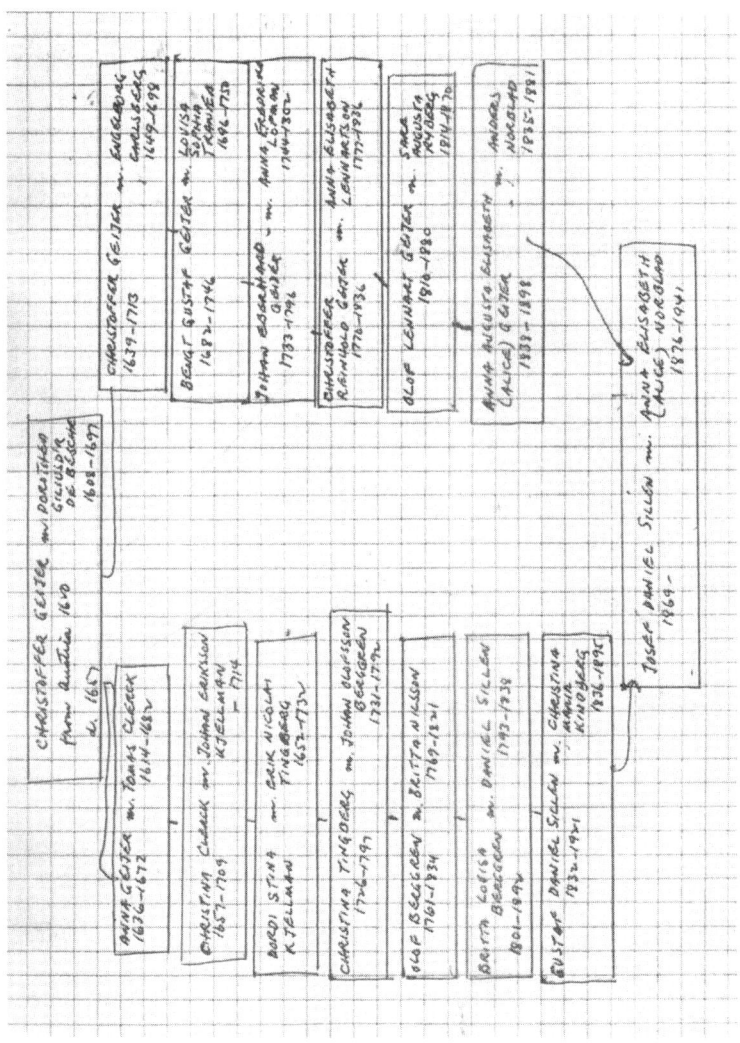

Chart drawn by Arne Pettersen, showing the common ancestry of Daniel Sillén and Alice Norblad.

CHAPTER 3

Ingrid Remembers: My Early Years

"Her temperament changes like April..."

My mother began her recording with memories of her early childhood:

"I have a letter that is very precious to me. My father wrote it to my oldest brother Gösta, who was away at school in Uddevalla [a larger town, approximately 40 miles southeast of Gesäter in the province of Västergötland]. He wrote it the same day I was born, and this is what he says:

'At 5:15 this morning the expected happened. It was a little girl, and all went well and quick. A little after four o'clock, I was awakened by Anna [Ingrid's eldest sister, 13 years old at the time]. At 4:20 I woke up Rönqvist [the caretaker], and as soon as he was ready, he ran to Rölanda [a neighboring town] to get the midwife. At 5:20, the midwife arrived. But as I told you, the baby had come five minutes earlier. Wilma [Rönqvist's wife] was present, but she had never been at a delivery before, so she wasn't much help. But she cut the cord. It was a good thing that I was not completely inexperienced. The little one is nice and cute and very healthy. And Greta [Ingrid's other sister, seven at the time] is very happy, as we all are, of course. Mama seems to be well and happy, too, and

we all have great reason to be thankful and to praise our Heavenly Father, Who, in His mercy, has helped us through this difficult time. He has heard our prayers and, in His mercy, done much more than we ever could hope for.'

"So I was born in the middle of the winter. This was November 27, 1915, during the first World War. It was a long, cold winter. I don't remember anything of that particular year, of course, but I was told that I was a difficult baby who cried a lot! We had no running water in the house at that time, and my sister told me that she had to carry water buckets from a well down a hill, and climbing up the icy hill, she often slipped and spilled the water and had to start all over again! We lived in a red parsonage called Prästbo, which means 'minister's home.' It was located in Gesäter in the province of Dalsland in Sweden. The nature was very beautiful with hills and meadows and trees.

"The house was small, but it was very comfortable. We had a living room, which was rather large, and inside there was a bedroom where my mother slept, and I used to sleep there, too. We had a dining room; my father's study, where he usually slept; and a kitchen. Upstairs we had two bedrooms, one for the boys and one for the girls.

"In each room except the kitchen we had a wood stove that went from the floor up to the ceiling, covered with tiles. These stoves were quite decorative and nice looking. They kept the heat and were very comfortable. We had an iron stove in the kitchen.

"It was a lot of work to cut the wood for all of these stoves. The boys did that, and when I was older I helped by carrying wood in a wheelbarrow. I think that may be why I have such long arms. Anyway, that's the way it was. It was a nice, quiet life, nothing fancy, but everyone was happy.

Young Ingrid in front of "Prästbo."

"We got milk from the caretaker, who managed the land that belonged to the parsonage. Milk was not pasteurized in those days. It would be delivered by one of his daughters in a pail. We poured it into bowls and put them in a pantry, as we didn't have any refrigeration. It stood there until the cream rose to the top, which was used for coffee, whipping cream and stuff like that. Sometimes when you came to the bottom of the

bowl, the milk was a little bit gray. Those cows were not terribly clean! That was no problem. We survived.

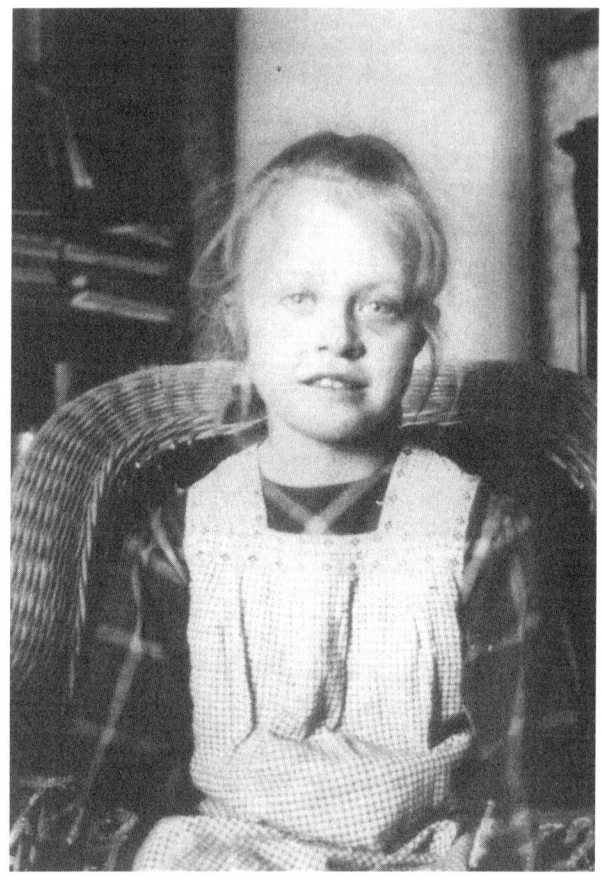

Ingrid as a young girl (undated)

"My father's name was Daniel Sillén. He was a Lutheran minister. He was born on April 8, 1869 and lived until March 29, 1950. He was then nearly eighty-one years old, and he had been a minister in our congregation for fifty-two years. He was very strict, and I was almost scared of him when I was little. But people respected him and liked him a lot, because he had a very good heart.

Daniel Sillen (1948)

"He always kept a first aid kit in his study, and often a farmer would stop in with an injured finger or leg and ask my father to take a look at it. If it wasn't too serious, my father would cleanse and bandage the wound. If he thought it was too much for him to handle, he sent him to the doctor. But farmers would always stop at the parsonage first. That was cheaper and quicker than to travel to the doctor who lived about twelve miles away. Most farmers had no cars in those days. They traveled by horse and buggy.

"My father was very musical. He had a beautiful voice and always chanted in church. He also played the flute. He had four sisters and three brothers. They were also very musical and played various instruments. They were all born in my home, since my grandfather was a minister there before my father.

"It was typical of my father to ask about some person you might talk about: 'Is he musical?' followed by, 'Is he interested in church?' He also loved to travel. Often on a Monday morning he would tell my mother, 'I have to get out. I'm leaving for a trip.' When my mother asked, 'Where are you going?' he would respond, 'I don't know, I'll call you tonight!' He had several minister friends in the area and they would get together and discuss religion and politics.

"My mother, Alice Norblad, was a wonderful person. Everybody in the congregation loved her. Often some old lady would come walking by and present my mother with eggs or butter or something similar from her farm. She might have walked a long time and be tired. My mother always took time out to sit down to talk and have a cup of coffee with her visitor, no matter how busy she might have been. She also helped in the homes, when babies arrived.

"I remember one morning when I woke up that Mother was already dressed and very cheerful. And she told me, 'Augusta had a baby girl last night.'

'How do you know?' I asked.

'I was there,' she replied.

"On the way to get the midwife with his horse and buggy, Augusta's husband had stopped at the parsonage and asked my mother to go over and stay with his wife until they came back. So she did. But the baby was in a *hurry, and when the midwife got there, the baby had already arrived! My mother had taken care of everything! She had no nursing training but always knew what to do.*

Anna Elisabeth (Alice) Sillén nee Norblad

"Mother loved flowers and plants. We had a porch where she grew many different varieties of geraniums. People often asked how she got them to bloom year around. 'I talk to them,' she said. She was also in charge of flowers and a vegetable garden outside, as well as our flock of chickens.

"I remember certain people from my childhood. One was an old man by the name of Alfred. He lived way up in the woods in a little house. I remember that it had grass growing on the roof, and I thought that was beautiful. He was not quite normal. He was a little behind, but he was very friendly and very helpful. Everybody in the congregation knew him. He had some time ago had an accident where he had lost his right hand, but he had sort of a hook. He was very handy, and he always helped my mother in the garden, digging and weeding and so on, and she used to call him her right hand. And I thought that was very funny because he didn't have a right hand! He only had a left hand!

"I had two brothers and two sisters. I was the youngest. My brother Gösta, born in 1899, was the oldest, and we all teased him about being born in another century. He became a missionary in Africa, where he died much too young in 1931. My sister Anna, born in 1902, married a minister, Carl Törnqvist, and my sister Greta, born in 1908, married his brother Bertil, also a minister. My brother Erik was born in 1904, and he, too, became a minister.

"I have a little notebook in which my father wrote poems when I had birthdays. One is from the day I was four years old, and I'll try to translate it here:

> 'My little Ingrid is four years old and does not understand much.
> Her temperament changes like April: sometimes tears and sometimes laughter.
> But she wants to be good and daily prays for that.
> She hopes to be a comfort for her parents when she grows up!

'And when the rest have left the nest and settled all over the world,
Then she will stay home with mother and father.
It will take a long time 'til she is grown.'

"I suppose in a way I disappointed my parents, as I left them and settled farther away than any of my sisters or brothers.

"Sundays were very quiet days in my home. Of course we always went to church, which was located high up on a hill. It took us about fifteen minutes to walk. My father had very long one-hour sermons, and it was difficult to sit still. We children had to sit in the front pew to be a good example for the rest of the congregation. I'll never forget the shame and humiliation I felt when once my father called out from the pulpit, 'Ingrid, sit still!'

"All of the women sat on the left side of the church and the men on the right. In the winter time, we sat near the wood stove to keep warm. Sometimes we brought a blanket to put over our legs.

"There was holy communion the first Sunday in the month. The Sunday before that my father would conduct an examination on the sermon or Luther's Catechism. It was always difficult to get anybody to answer. If I didn't or wouldn't or couldn't answer some questions, I would get a lecture when I got home.

"The old women usually wore black going to church, and they wore black silk shawls on their heads. The back of the pews in church had a piece of wood across the top which cut into your back if you leaned back. People who went to church every Sunday had a distinct mark on the back of their Sunday coat from this! On the way home from church we were supposed to walk quietly, thinking about the sermon and not talking to anybody.

The church in Gesäter, built in 1795.

The interior of the church (from a current postcard)

"No unnecessary work was to be done on Sunday. Shoes had to be polished and potatoes peeled on Saturday. We never had company on Sunday. We could never read a newspaper, sew or knit on Sunday. I was allowed to take walks in the woods and pick flowers, which I liked to do.

"My schooling was rather sporadic. I went to grammar school about six years. Then my father decided it would be better for me if he tutored me at home. He especially insisted I learn German, which at that time was not taught in the grammar school. It was not a happy situation, and I missed not being with other children. Later it was difficult for me to get into Uddevalla Flickskola, a high school for girls, about 40 miles away, where I studied for a couple of years. I then lived with two old ladies who took in boarders.

"Before that, though, I was confirmed together with another girl and two boys. We had public examination in church which lasted **two hours!** I had a black confirmation dress. My father would not allow a white dress which later could be used for parties. You had to wear black when you took communion.

"As I mentioned earlier, we had no conveniences, for instance, no washing machine. Underwear and light wash we did by hand. But when we had a big wash with sheets and tablecloths, it was quite an undertaking. A couple of girls would come in the morning to help. We had a smaller house on the property where there was a big room where the washing took place. Each girl had a barrel with clothes that had been soaked in soap over night. I helped, too. We each had a washboard and rubbed the clothes up and down on it. After several hours of this we often had sores across our fingers. Then the clothes were put in a huge kettle and boiled in lye for an hour or so. When this was done, the caretaker would come with a horse and a flat wagon on which we placed all the barrels of clothes. Then they were transported down to the river. There we rinsed the clothes in the river and with a wooden paddle banged them against a rock to get rid of the soap and lye. Sometimes the water was cold, depending upon the time of the year, and our fingers would get stiff. When this procedure was finished, the clean clothes were transported home again. Usually we left them in the barrels until the next day. Then we used a hand wringer to remove the rinse water and hung everything up to dry. If it was too cold to hang outside, we hung the wash on lines in the attic. Once a little mouse had chewed holes on a tablecloth all along the center where it had been across the line! I would probably have cut out the center piece and made a seam. Not my mother! She carefully darned every little hole.

"When the clothes were dry, they were taken down and the sheets and tablecloths folded by hand. My mother was very particular about her linen closet. Every sheet and tablecloth had an embroidered monogram. One of her favorite expressions was 'It doesn't show how long it took, but it shows how well it was done.'

"We usually had a girl helping my mother with the housework and cooking. One of these was my special friend. Her name was Sofie. She helped care for me when I was very young, and I remember if someone scolded me, she would always defend me. *After a nap sometimes I would feel out of sorts. Sofie would understand and take time out to hold me in her lap until I felt better. Later she lived with her mother in a little house about an hour's walk away. Every Christmas Eve I would walk over to her house and we would exchange Christmas gifts. We kept in touch after I came here. She would write such nice letters telling everything from the home front, who got married, who had a baby, who had died, etc.*

The Sillén family, ca. 1920. Back row, left to right: Erik, Greta and Anna. Front row, left to right: Gösta, Daniel, Alice and Ingrid.

"When I went to Sweden in 1973, I visited her in a very nice nursing home. She always seemed happy and satisfied. On her dresser, I noticed a picture of me, taken when I was four years old.

"Christmas was a very special time during my childhood. The preparations started early in December. Every day in the Swedish calendar has a name. December 9 was Anna day and on that day, the Christmas preparations were supposed to start. One of the things was to soak 'Lutefisk.' This was a big dried fish, I think something like cod fish. First it was soaked in cold water a couple of days. Then it was soaked in lye for about a week. This made the fish swell and get thick. Then it was rinsed off and soaked in cold water, which had to be changed every day to get rid of the lye. For Christmas dinner it was cooked in salt water, being careful not to boil it. It was served with white sauce with salt and pepper and butter. It was considered a delicacy, but I think it was more a tradition. We also baked a lot of pepparkakor [gingerbread] and other cookies. Sometimes we got half a pig and then we made sausage, head cheese, ham and bacon. Some day before Christmas my father would take a walk out in the woods and select a Christmas tree. Then he would go to the farmer who owned the woods where the tree grew and ask if he could buy it. Of course the farmer would say, 'I'll give it to you, pastor, and I will bring it to the parsonage.' Thus we always had a very fresh Christmas tree, and it was always the most beautiful Christmas tree we had ever had. We had homemade ornaments and small real candles. We never had a fire. I guess the tree was so fresh it couldn't burn anyway! It was always placed in a corner of the living room.

"On Christmas Eve, after we had eaten a big dinner of lutefisk, smörgåsbord, coffee and cookies, the door to the living room was closed. After a short while the door opened, and father had lit all the candles on the tree! What a beautiful sight! At the foot of the tree was a clothes basket full of Christmas presents. But we couldn't open them yet! First father read the Christmas Gospel and a sermon.

"Usually we were all home for Christmas. My brothers who both were away most of the time were home on vacation. We never had luxurious presents, most of them homemade, but everybody was happy. We didn't have fancy wrapping paper, but brown paper was good, and we always used red sealing wax, which filled the house with a special Christmas aroma.

"I have a little notebook diary, where I wrote 'Christmas 1925' describing all the presents I received: 'From Father a picture of two sleigh riding children, two nice postcards, a piece of soap, two pencils, a small wooden bear and a box of raisins. Mother gave me a pair of stockings, this notebook and stationery. My big brother gave me a paint box and brush with a poem and a chocolate lamb. Erik gave me a wooden box he had made; inside were 100 biblical pictures, fifty from Erik, fifty from Greta. She also gave me a pin cushion she had before but she had made a new cover for it, two spools of thread, a measuring tape and a marzipan Santa. Anna was not with us that Christmas. She was in her own home, having had her first baby December 22nd. But she sent me a children's calendar, and my aunt sent me a candlestick with candles and shoes for my doll Berta and a dress she had knit for the doll. Sofie gave me a piece of material, so I made out okay!

A contemporary picture of "Prästbo," a private home since 1988.

"We had to go to bed early on Christmas Eve in order to be up at up 6 o'clock Christmas morning to go to the dawn service Julottan in church. The ground was usually covered with snow, and people would travel to church in sleighs pulled by horses. The church was lit by real candles in the chandeliers. It was a glorious sight, a wonderful feeling I'll never forget. We always sang 'Så Skön Går Morgonstjärnan'('How Brightly Shines the Morning Star'). The church was always filled on Christmas. When we came home we had time to look at and enjoy our Christmas presents. We also observed a second Christmas day which was a church holiday. Not many people came to church then and Father was unhappy.

"The following days we usually had company or went visiting friends. There were some minister families living in neighboring congregations and we would travel by horse and sleigh to visit and there was always so much food to eat.

"One summer, when I was about sixteen or seventeen, I went on a long bicycle trip together with an older friend Signe. She really was Greta's friend. My parents felt better if I had an older friend accompanying me. I had an old bicycle handed down from my older sister, not in very good condition. We had a marvelous time and traveled eighty Swedish miles in 14 days, about 480 miles. What a wonderful way to see nature! We slept in haylofts and hostels but also visited some relations on the way, so we could get a bath and sleep in a bed. It must have been rough on poor Signe, since I always had wild ideas. Once we stopped at a lake, I found a rowboat and started rowing out with Signe and me. She was scared, because she couldn't swim. I just laughed at her! What a naughty girl!"

CHAPTER 4

Whence the Pettersens

Go west, young man.

Horace Greeley

The Pettersen family lineage has been traced back to a Swede by the name of Per Månsson, who was born in Värmland in 1762. (We only know the name of Per's father through a logical deduction. It had to be Måns!) Per married a woman by the name of Margrethe Persdotter, and on February 1, 1795 she gave birth to a son, whom they named Oluf. Following Swedish convention, his surname became Persson. Per died in 1811, a month before his forty-ninth birthday.

On October 20, 1813, just two and a half years after his father's death, eighteen-year-old Oluf married a woman by the name of Ingrid Eriksdotter. Their first child, a son, was born thirteen months later, on November 21, 1814. They named him Petter. Oluf proved to be an enterprising young man and achieved a level of prominence in his community. Over time he acquired a substantial amount of property, including at least three farms, and was elected as a *namndeman*, a judicial office slightly below the level of a judge.

On the day after Christmas in 1839, at the age of twenty-five, Petter married Ingrid Jonasdotter, the daughter of Jonas and Anna Torstenson, and they settled on one of his father's properties in the village of Kalfskog, Tveda Parish, in Värmland. Over the next fifteen years they had five sons – Anders, born in 1841; Johannes, 1844; Erik, 1846; Oscar, 1849; and Janne, 1854. All adopted the surname Petterson (literally son of Petter and using the Swedish "son"). Little is known about Anders, except that he never married and that he died in February of 1875 at the age of thirty-three. Erik died not long after his thirteenth birthday. The three remaining brothers all were educated as tailors in Sweden.

In 1870, Johannes moved to Christiania (now Oslo), where business prospects appeared to be far better than at home. Oscar and Janne followed their brother about five years later, renting a room together in Christiania in 1875 and registering as tailors.

The following year, on June 25, 1876, at the age of twenty-six, Oscar was married in Christiania to another native of Värmland, Charlotta Wallin, who was from the town of Glava in Arvika parish. Shortly thereafter, Oscar left the tailoring business and took a position as a prison guard. In 1882 he got a job as a mailman at the Christiania post office, a position he was to hold for the rest of his life.

Oscar and Charlotta had six children, three of whom did not survive to their first birthday: Johan Samuel, born August 15, 1877, lived seven and a half months; Charlotte Marie, born January 21, 1879, lived just six and a half months; and Oscar Adolph, born April 8, 1885, was not quite ten months old when he died. The three surviving children – Samuel, born June 3, 1880; Karl Stefanus, born August 2, 1882, who was to go by his middle name, Stefanus; and Hanna Elisabeth, born March 8, 1887 – adopted the Norwegian spelling of their last name, Pettersen. Tragically, Charlotta died on October 27, 1889, at the age of just forty, when her youngest child Hanna was only two and a half years old. Oscar remarried a year later to Maria Karlsdatter, but he himself only lived another five years. By this time, Samuel and Stefanus were fifteen and thirteen, respectively, and both had to find employment.

Charlotta and Oscar

Janne and Sophie
(apparently taken in winter!

On February 8, 1879, at the age of twenty-four, Oscar's younger brother Janne also married a fellow Swede, Sophia (Sophie) Olsson. They had five children: Frantz Oskar, born November 18, 1879; Lydia Marie, born August 16, 1881; Johan Ragnvald, born December 11, 1883; Paul Stefanus, born March 21, 1886; and Ruth Sofie, born June 23, 1888. Sophia died on January 6, 1891, at the tender age of thirty-nine. Her oldest child was just eleven and her youngest, two and a half.

Six years later, on April 14, 1897, Janne remarried, to Constanse Andersen. He fathered six more children: Petrus (1898), Ingrid (1900), Ester (1902), Georg (1904), Rolf (1906) and Gudrun (1910). Seven of Janne's eleven children adopted the Norwegian spelling of their surname, Pettersen, but Frantz, Georg, Rolf and Gudrun retained the Swedish Petterson.

Family lore says that Janne's clientele included the famed Nordic explorer, Roald Amundsen, and that, with left over fabric, he made clothing for his children. With eleven children, he certainly would need a lot of leftovers! The picture below suggests that these remnants were not too shabby!

Janne with his second wife Constanse, their first child Petrus, and Janne's five children by Sophie. Back row, left to right: Paul, Johan, Frantz and Lydia. Front row, left to right, Constanse, Petrus, Ruth and Janne.

A simplified family tree is presented on the following page.

Whence the Pettersens

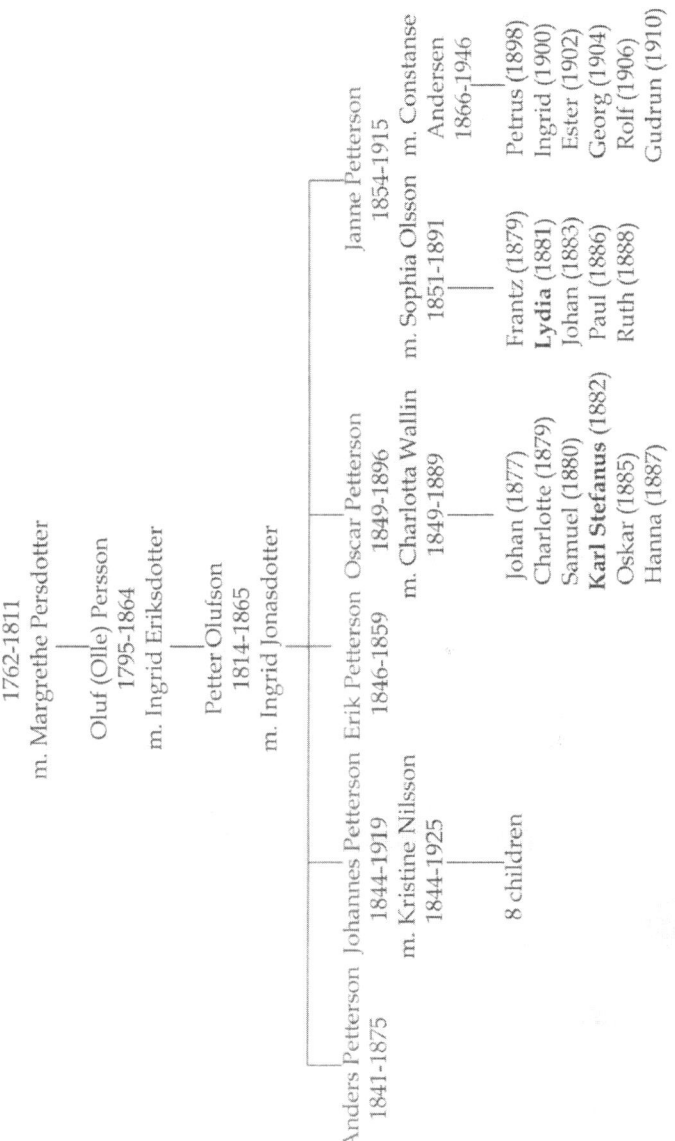

CHAPTER 5

Stefanus and Lydia

"Acquaint now thyself with him, and be at peace: thereby good shall come unto thee." Job 22:21

After his father's death in 1896, thirteen-year-old Stefanus found a job as an errand boy for the city newspaper, *Aftenposten*. He worked there until 1898. Then sixteen, beginning as an apprentice machinist, he developed his skills in different workshops in Christiania and Bergen, successfully passing the machinist's exam in 1903 and the electrical technology exam in 1904.

Young Stefanus (undated)

With these qualifications, he hired on as a shipboard engineer and served aboard several vessels in the Far East for two and a half years. He sent home sufficient funds to pay for his sister Hanna's education at Kristiania Teachers School.

Stefanus in Hong Kong - 1906

Stefanus arrived back in Christiania on January 10, 1907. Now twenty-four years old, he promptly began to call on his cousin Lydia, Janne's daughter. On more than one occasion he asked her to marry him. She was very much in doubt, but Stefanus was persistent, repeating to himself, "Tomorrow is another day."

One day, while she was reading her Bible, Lydia's eyes happened to fall on Job 22:21: "Acquaint now thyself with him, and be at peace: thereby good shall come unto thee." With this assurance, she then accepted Stefanus' proposal.

Lydia and Stefanus on their wedding day

Stefanus and Lydia were married on February 16, 1907, just thirty-seven days after his return to Oslo, thereby setting a family precedent for brief courtships. Their first child, a son, was born fifty-one weeks later, and they christened him Ragnar. Each of them had a sentimental reason for the name. Stefanus' last ship was the D/S *Kong Ragnar*, named in honor of an ancient Viking king, and Lydia sought to honor her brother, Johan Ragnvald.

Fifteen months later, Lydia gave birth to their second child and first daughter in the city of Drammen, just south of Oslo, where Stefanus had taken a position as an engineer at a paper mill. They named her Lydia Marie, after her mother. The family then moved to the city of Trondheim on Norway's west coast, where Stefanus had found employment as an engineer at the newly built Trondheim Technical High School. Arne, the third of their children, was born there on the auspicious date of January 11, 1911 (1/11/11). Over the next seven years in Trondheim, Stefanus and Lydia became the parents of four more children, three sons and a daughter – Henry (1912), Gudrun (1913), Birger (1916) and Torbjørn (1918).

In 1918, when he and Lydia had been married barely eleven years, Stefanus took a position with the University in Oslo. They moved there at the end of October with their seven children, the oldest of whom was ten-year-old Ragnar and the youngest, their eight-month-old son Torbjørn.

Arne recalled that their arrival in Oslo coincided with the Spanish flu epidemic which was ravaging the world. Because their furniture had not yet come, the family found temporary quarters at the University, sleeping on mattresses on the floor. They all took sick, one after the other. Gudrun was the most severely afflicted and was hospitalized for months.

Family photo, ca. 1914 or 1915. Left to right: Lydia, Petrus (Lydia's step-brother), Gudrun, Lydia, Henry, Arne, Stefanus and Ragnar.

Lydia bore three more children after the family's move to Oslo: Astri in 1919, Oddvar in 1920 and Johannes on January 11, 1922, which coincided with Arne's eleventh birthday.

Stefanus' professional reputation and influence continued to increase during the 1920s. In addition to his position at the University, he held equity interest in one company and board membership in another. But the story he liked to tell concerned a particularly memorable encounter. The famous Norwegian explorer and diplomat Fridtjof Nansen had been selected to receive the 1922 Nobel Peace Prize for his considerable work on behalf of refugees after the First

World War. The award ceremony was to be held in the Aula, or Great Hall, at the University of Oslo. Stefanus stood outside on the stairs, greeting important guests, including the King, as they arrived. Finally, Nansen came running up the steps, concerned that he might be late. He asked whether there were many people inside. With a smile, Stefanus replied that he thought there was one place left.

The following year, in 1923, Stefanus managed to purchase an apartment building in downtown Christiania, a short distance from the University and the royal palace. The address was Huitfeldtsgate 12. In addition to providing space for his large family, he planned to use it as a source of income after his retirement and as security for Lydia if he should happen to predecease her.

Huitfeldtsgate 12, as it appeared in 1987

In 1924, the year in which the Norwegian capital reverted to its original name of Oslo, Stefanus was named chairman of Kristiania Maskinistforening, the association of professional engineers in Oslo. He held that position for two years while continuing to work at the University.

Lydia's brothers Johan and Paul emigrated to the United States in 1908 and settled initially in Minneapolis. Johan Americanized his name to John, and then both brothers adopted the surname of Ragnvald, John's middle name. Their sister Ruth, who appears later in this story, also came to the United States. She, too, adopted the surname Ragnvald and settled in Chicago. Frantz died in Norway just before Christmas in 1918 at the age of 39, possibly a casualty of the Spanish flu pandemic. This left Lydia the only one among Sophia's surviving children to remain in Norway.

In 1909, with the objective of settling less fertile lands out West, the U.S. Congress passed the Enlarged Homestead Act, which increased the amount of land a homesteader could claim from 160 to 320 acres. Seizing this opportunity, Paul traveled west to Montana and staked a claim in Garfield, north of Miles City, in the eastern part of the state. There he met Olga Marie Olsen, whom he married on October 31, 1915. They had three children: Esther (1916), Bernice (1917) and Robert (1921).

John never married. Bernice recalled that, while still in Minneapolis, he contracted tuberculosis, and Ruth sent him to live with Paul and his family in Montana. Paul managed to get John admitted to a sanitarium in Deer Lodge, in the western part of the state, where he recovered and became an X-ray technician. John lived in Deer Lodge until his death in 1965.

John and Paul Ragnvald

Chapter 6

"Iron Brain"

*If we encounter a man of rare intellect,
we should ask him what books he reads.*
Ralph Waldo Emerson

Stefanus' and Lydia's son Arne was an especially precocious child. Older family members recalled that at the age of four he would pick up the newspaper, and they soon realized that he was actually reading it. He went on to excel in school, to such an extent that he acquired the nickname of "Iron Brain."

Arne's education was accelerated because of a freak accident. When he was five years old, he suffered a severe leg fracture in a sledding mishap. As he later told it, the leg was set incorrectly, and when the cast was removed, the doctors refractured it intentionally so that it could heal properly. As a result, he remained on crutches for nearly two years. Even later in life, he enjoyed showing off his dexterity and ability to climb stairs on crutches.

With apparently nothing else to do but read and study, Arne skipped two grades in school and was ultimately graduated from a two-year business college at the age of sixteen. He obtained an entry level job with an Oslo based shipping company, Fearnley and Eger, where he caught the eye of one of the owners, Thomas Fearnley, and moved up the ladder quickly.

Among his many interests, Arne was fascinated by his family's genealogy and sought to learn as much as he could about his forebears. He knew that his family had actually moved to Norway from Sweden in the late 1800s, and he found that the best sources of information were the parish records of local churches in the family's ancestral home of Värmland in the western part of the country. His travels eventually took him to a rural farming community in Dalsland called Gesäter (pronounced YEH-say-ter), where he introduced himself to the pastor, Reverend Daniel Sillén. During his visit, he met Pastor Sillén's youngest daughter Ingrid, a nursing student who happened to be home at the time.

Arne at seventeen (1928)

In 1937, at the age of twenty-six, Arne's company relocated him to the United States to help establish an American presence. His assignment was to first set up a branch office in New York, then one in New Orleans and one in San Francisco, taking six months for each, after which he would return to Norway. As it happened, the last two legs of his assignment were never to materialize. At the time of his departure, as best as we have been able to ascertain, he had seen Ingrid just twice.

Arne's travel from Oslo to New York was by no means direct. He was issued a passport in Oslo on August 11, 1937, good only for the passage to the United States. He sailed on one of Fearnley and Eger's cargo ships, the *M/S Ferncliff*[3], leaving on or about that same day. His passport shows a stop in Copenhagen from August 15th through the 23rd; a stamp from "Passkontroll" at the Østfold Canal, near Halden, Norway on August 30; a stop in Bremen, Germany from October 21st to the 24th, where he purchased 75 ReichMarks in travelers checks; and his arrival in Baltimore on November 15. There he was granted a visa for one year. Other details of his ninety-six day journey remain a mystery, but it may be that during the first two and a half months of intra-European sailing, the *Ferncliff* was picking up various cargoes for their ultimate destination in the United States. If so, this would have given Arne an excellent opportunity to gain familiarity with the ship's operations and to establish valuable contacts in each of the ports which he visited. He finally arrived in New York on November 17.

Over the next two years, Arne established a New York office for his company in lower Manhattan at 39 Broadway and leased an apartment in a complex called "The Narrows" in the Bay Ridge section of Brooklyn, which was home to a thriving Scandinavian community. Its address was No. 1 74th Street, overlooking the Shore Parkway, the Verrazano

Narrows and New York Harbor. Among its advantages was easy access to lower Manhattan via the B.M.T line of the New York subway system. He also became an active member at nearby Trinity Lutheran Church, pastored by the Reverend Paul Scaer.

During the first two to three years after his arrival in the United States, Arne continued to travel. His passport documents at least one trip back to Europe in November 1938, with stops in both London and Göteborg.[4] In July of 1939 he sent a postcard to his brother Ragnar with a photograph of Victoria Falls, which he said he had taken on his most recent trip to Africa.

In another card mailed to Ragnar on his birthday, February 8, 1940, Arne obviously had more than a premonition of what lay ahead. He wrote: "[This is] sent in troublesome times. So far, New York has only been slightly involved, i.e., with war traffic and exports...Bombers to England. One lighter sank off Staten Island. And the question arose, but was hushed down: Accident or sabotage?"

Later that year, on October 5, as a consequence of the Nazi occupation of Norway, Arne was given full power of attorney for all of Fearnley and Eger's affairs. By the start of the war the firm's fleet had grown to twenty-two ships, with an aggregate capacity of more than 155,000 deadweight tonnage. He was not yet thirty years old.

Six months earlier, with his career on a rapid upward trajectory, Arne realized that something was missing in his life. Or perhaps it was someone. He decided to do something about it.

CHAPTER 7

Ingrid Remembers: Growing Up

"Do you have to go all the way to America and marry a Norwegian?"

While Arne was establishing himself in the United States, Ingrid completed nursing school. She took a position at Sahlgrenske Hospital in Göteborg, about two hours south of Gesäter. However, when her mother Alice fell ill, she left her job to come home and care for her, as her older siblings were all married. In April of 1940, with continental Europe at war and Scandinavia threatened, Ingrid received a letter from Arne that set off the chain of events recounted in the pages that follow. Her recording continues:

"In the spring of 1936, when I was twenty years old, I started nursing school in Göteborg. That was very hard and thorough training for three years. We worked twelve-hour shifts, had one afternoon off every week and one day a month. We had a uniform: a light blue cotton dress, shirtwaist, long sleeves, starched white collar and cuffs, a white bib apron, black stockings and shoes. For special occasions we wore a navy blue dress. We also had a navy coat and a hat with a veil. We almost looked like nuns! We had to wear our uniforms even on days off.

"I graduated in the spring of 1939 together with about twenty-eight other girls. And then we got a white

cap, with a band under the chin to tie a bow, signifying that we were a full-fledged nurse. And that year I continued to work in the hospital as an assistant to one of the head nurses. I was paid ninety kronor per month, and that was fantastic. Of course, money went a little farther in those days than it does today. But even so, it was the first time that I earned my own money.

Graduation from nursing school. Ingrid is in center of back row.

"In the fall – I think it was about the beginning of December – I contracted scarlet fever. I had been working one night, substituting for another nurse in the maternity ward, and I had a terrific sore throat. When I went to the doctor in the morning, he discovered that I had strep throat or scarlet fever, and I caught hell from the nurse and doctors, because I had worked in maternity. They had to isolate the whole ward. And I was so sick and tired, I couldn't care less. And then they put me in the epidemic hospital in isolation. I think I was there for about a month. I was there over Christmas. I remember that Greta came to visit me. She was standing on a stepladder outside the window and waved at me. I had a roommate, and she got complications afterwards. She got rheumatic fever. We didn't have penicillin in those days. I don't remember which year that was discovered, but anyway, I had no complications. Afterwards they sent me home for a month to be in isolation, and I was happy to be home.

"Right before I took sick, I had almost been coaxed into accepting a position as a night nurse on the surgical floors. The head nurse, or supervisor, convinced me that it would be very educational for me to get this position. I told her that I didn't feel qualified, because I was not experienced enough, and I also said, 'I can't sleep on days.' 'Well,' she said, 'you'll learn to sleep days.' So I applied for the job, and I got it. But the year was cut short because of my having to go home to my father and mother in January for a month.

"Then in early 1940 I started working as a night nurse in the hospital. The hospital was very old. It had a terribly long corridor with a tiled floor. From the corridor there were pavilions going out on each side. Each pavilion had two wards, one on the first floor and one on the second. I was in charge of five wards, two at the beginning of the corridor, one in the middle and two at the end. Each ward had forty patients. There was one nursing student in each ward. It seemed that whenever I was at one end of the corridor, a light would go on at the other end. I was forever running back and forth in this slippery hall, and my legs and feet were aching. So I *brought in my bicycle and started riding back and forth. There was no other traffic. I was completely alone in the hall...until one morning I spotted a doctor. While riding I said, 'Good morning, doctor.' He started laughing and said 'That is very sensible!' And I heard that, even after I had left, the night nurses continued to ride their bicycles.*

"I especially remember one night I had been working that I was so tired in the morning, but I was very happy that I was going to be off the following night. I had been invited to dinner by some friends about six o'clock that day. I didn't set the alarm, figuring that I would wake up in plenty of time. I went to bed, and it was wonderful to know that I was going to be off the following night. Lo and behold, I woke up at six o'clock and I thought, 'Oops, I overslept!' So I called my friend and said, 'I'm awfully sorry, but I overslept, and I'll come as soon as I can.' She started laughing, and I said, 'What's so funny?' She said, 'You were supposed to come yesterday!' So I had slept through one day, one night and another day, thirty hours or so. So I lost a whole day, but I felt rested. I couldn't do that today."

****

From his youth Ingrid's oldest brother Gösta had dreams of becoming a missionary, and he excelled in his studies. After being ordained a Lutheran minister and then completing a year of language courses in England, he set out for southern Africa in early 1927. Prior to his departure, he met and fell in love with Esther Helldén. Esther was the eldest daughter of

Adolf and Alma Helldén, who had served as missionaries in South Africa before returning to Sweden for their children's education.

On March 15, 1928, a year after Gösta's arrival in South Africa, he and Esther were married at the Oskarberg mission station in Natal, where she had been born. Their first child, whom they named Carl-Erik, was born on December 13, 1928, but he lived just a day. On September 2, 1930, Esther delivered a daughter, whom they named Anne-Marie. Just a year later, Gösta contracted a fatal tropical disease. He died on October 26, 1931, at the tender age of thirty-two. His grieving widow sent a telegram to notify the family: "My Gösta was called into the joy of the Lord on Monday evening." The telegram was not received in Sweden until October 29, the very day that Esther's younger sister Ruth was being married to Gösta's younger brother Erik.

Like his brother, his father and so many ancestors before him, Erik was ordained as a Lutheran minister in Karlstad in 1927. After serving for a year as an assistant to his Uncle Gustaf in the town of Grums, he was called first to the parish in the town of Holm and then, in 1934, to Brålanda, a small rural village near the southwest shore of Lake Vänern. He was to serve there for more than thirty-five years. By 1939, Ruth had already borne the first four of their ten children.

During Ingrid's tenure at Sahlgrenske Hospital, her sisters Anna and Greta were living in Göteborg with their families. Anna had actually been the first of the Sillén siblings to wed, marrying Rev. Carl Törnqvist, who was exactly ten years her senior, on July 9, 1924, when she was only twenty-two. On April

6, 1932, Greta married Carl's younger brother Bertil, who was also an ordained Lutheran minister. Anna and Carl already had four children – Sven in 1925, Carl-Erik in 1928, Hedvig in 1930 and Johannes in 1932; and Greta and Bertil had three – Barbro in 1933, Stig in 1935 and Gerd in 1937.

Throughout her years in Göteborg, both in nursing school and during her employment at the hospital, Ingrid visited Greta, Bertil and their growing family whenever she could.

As the youngest child, now a qualified registered nurse with no other family responsibilities, there was a tacit expectation that Ingrid would be available to care for her parents. But in 1940 her life was about to change profoundly. She continues:

"On April 9 of that year I received a letter from Arne Pettersen in the U.S.A.! While reading this letter, in which he proposed to me, I got news over the radio that Germany had invaded Norway. I sure had mixed emotions! I knew the answer would be 'Yes.' We had only met twice, but I guess there was a spark. I went to the telegraph station and wanted to send a telegram to the U.S.A. simply saying 'YES.' But that was not permitted. The war was on and a secret code was needed. So the wording of the telegram became rather cold, something like 'Agree to marriage'! But I suppose that was satisfactory.

"This was the start of regular correspondence between the U.S.A. and Sweden. Most letters were censored, but once in a while we were lucky. For instance, one letter contained my engagement ring, and *another a lovely diamond cross, a gift for my 25th birthday, and that letter was not censored. I'm still wearing it. I also got various suggestions about how to travel to America – via Japan, Siberia, etc.*

"*I continued working all that year. Sweden remained neutral, but Göteborg was near the Norwegian border. We had blackouts in the city, and the atmosphere was very tense. We were not allowed to go out after dark, but some of the girls did, anyway.*"

Unbeknownst to Ingrid, Arne's 22-year-old younger brother Torbjørn had left Oslo on the passenger liner *Stavangerfjord* bound for New York on April 8, 1940, the day before the German invasion. The ship was just passing north of Scotland when they heard the news. He later recounted that the ship carried four categories of passengers: (1) German Jews, relieved that they had escaped; (2) worried fathers who asked the captain to turn back so that they could be with their families in Norway; (3) people venting their anger against the Germans and Norwegian quislings;[5] and (4) those like him with tight fists in their pockets, looking angry but not talking much.

Torbjørn had studied medicine in Oslo since 1936. Upon arriving in the United States, he contacted the Norwegian consulate asking for advice. In order to achieve an active role in the Norwegian liberation forces he was asked to conclude his medical studies in Toronto, not far from the Norwegian air force training camp 'Little Norway.' He was formally inducted into the Norwegian Air Force on September 10, 1940 and earned his medical diploma from Toronto in 1942.

While completing his studies, he would find a number of opportunities to visit his brother in New York.

Ingrid continued: *"Arne had wanted to come home to Norway and Sweden so we would get married in my father's church. But the war put a stop to that, so somehow I had to get to the U.S.A. But I couldn't leave my job and my mother who was ailing. As the youngest, I was supposed to stay home and be a comfort to my parents. At the end of 1940 I quit my job and went home to stay with my parents for a while. I did not realize it then, how hard it must have been for them to have the youngest leave to live so far away. My father said, 'Isn't there anyone in Sweden good enough for you? Do you have to go all the way to America and marry a Norwegian?'*

"My parents had met Arne a couple of times, so they knew I would be okay. I had never met Arne's relatives in Norway, and it was impossible to travel there because of the war. In the spring of 1941 I talked to Arne's father on the phone, and he said to me, 'You better get over there as soon as possible.'

"Meanwhile, my mother's condition deteriorated. She had a very bad case of arthritis, and it had also affected her heart. It was difficult for me to make a decision. I prayed a lot about it, and I hoped that I would get an answer, that someone would make the decision for me somehow, but my heart was in the U.S.A."

Aware of Ingrid's inner conflict over this, Alice, despite her illness, encouraged her daughter to continue to pray and to follow her heart. Ingrid continued:

"In May I went back to Göteborg to get my visa and passport, just in case there would be some opening for travel. I also went to the Transatlantic Ship Company to see a man whom Arne knew, Gunnar Carlsson. I asked him whether there was any way of getting over to America. He just looked at me as though I were crazy. Our conversation went something like this:

"He asked, 'And why in the world do you want to go to America now?'

'Well, I am going to get married!'

'You are absolutely crazy!'

'Yes, I know, but can you tell me if there is any possibility?'

"He looked at me and said, 'Well, I'll tell you, we have a cargo ship that is leaving next week, and there is one passage left which was canceled yesterday!'

"I felt that was the answer to my prayers. So I said, 'Okay I'll take that!' And then I found a telephone and called Arne and said, 'I'm leaving next week!'

"It was quiet on the other end, and I said, 'Don't you want me to come?'

'Oh, yes, yes, I'll be waiting for you.'

"Then I bought two trunks, went home, packed and quickly said my goodbyes. It was difficult, but it was better that it wasn't too drawn out. I was convinced that

I was not going to settle in America, but that we would be coming home in a couple of years. So I said, 'I'll be back soon.'"

CHAPTER 8

American Bride

Good company makes the trip short.
(Danish proverb)

It is hard to overstate the perils of trans-Atlantic travel in the Spring of 1941. After Germany's invasion of Denmark and Norway on April 9, 1940, both the British and German navies blocked the Skaggerak, the strategically important strait between Norway and the southwest coast of Sweden and the Jutland peninsula of Denmark, which opens to the North Sea and, ultimately, the Atlantic. During the next two months, thirteen Swedish merchant ships were sunk in the Skaggerak, along with a number of smaller fishing vessels. Thus isolated, Sweden became dependent on trade with Germany and German-occupied countries.

Clearly alarmed by this, Swedish diplomats convinced Germany and England, after extensive negotiations, to allow passage of a few vessels, mainly to the United States – until the U.S. entry into the war – and neutral South American countries, particularly Argentina. These transports, called **lejdtrafiken**, "the escort traffic," were monitored by both powers. Despite Sweden's agreements with Germany and England, ten of these ships were sunk during the war. Sweden mainly imported petroleum products and agricultural produce and exported wood and paper products. Oil imports were severely restricted, to as little as ten percent of normal volumes. As the war progressed, strategic products such as rubber and metals were prohibited.[6] Just four ships per month were allowed to pass in and out of Göteborg, and both the British and the Germans retained the right to inspect them.

In May of 1941, one of those ships was the M/S *Remmaren*, a small cargo ship displacing 3,775 gross tons. Ingrid describes her departure:

"Our ship left Göteborg at four o'clock in the morning on May 21. It was a small cargo ship with only seventeen passengers. I shared a cabin with Anna-Lisa Montheli, who became one of my very best friends.

"In the afternoon of that day, we reached the southern coast of Norway, went through a mine field, and there we were halted by a German warship. A German officer came on board to inspect our passports. It was very tense. There were several Jewish refugees on board. But he let us go, and everyone breathed a sigh of relief.

"In our cabin, there was hung a large rubber contraption. It was a life saving suit, in case we were to capsize. It had a red flag in the pocket. Anna Lisa and I christened it, 'Svarte Rudolf.' Fortunately, we never had to use it.

"The trip was very exciting. I really enjoyed it. I had a ball. I had never been on a big trip like this before. It took fourteen days, but it was not without danger. We were on the ocean the same week that the Bismarck and the Hood went down.[7] We heard about it, and I can imagine how my parents must have felt.

"While hosting a dinner two days before we arrived in New York, the captain told us that two days earlier he had spotted two mines close to the ship. But now he said we would get to New York okay."

On June 5, 1941, the day after the arrival of the *Remmaren* in New York, the *Herald Tribune* chronicled its voyage in an article titled, "Swedish Ship In From War Zone On Debut Visit," with the sub-head, "17 on Board Tell How New Passenger Freighter Ran Mine Fields at Top Speed:"

> "The motorship Remmaren of the Swedish Transatlantic Line made her first visit to New York yesterday [after traveling at top] speed around floating mines in the North Sea. She is 3,500 gross tons of elegant passenger vessel and glorified freighter.
>
> "American and foreign naval architects have acclaimed her as one of the finest products of modern passenger-cargo vessel design. To this her seventeen passengers added their own praise, telling of $200 suites of living room and twin-bed cabins, with trunk rooms and large private baths that would cost $1,100 or more at peace-time prices on the giant luxury liners.
>
> "The suite occupied by Commodore O.W.E. Huldgren (sic), her master, who has been superintending engineer of eight of the thirty-two vessels owned by the line, appeared to ship news reporters to be more luxurious than those of commanders of liners ten times her size. Yet the Remmaren earns her keep. Like a lady's pocketbook, which can hold an astonishing

amount of miscellaneous articles, she was carrying 5,500 tons of general cargo, part of it destined for Havana and Vera Cruz.

"The $1,000,000 motor ship came up the upper bay cloaked in the early morning mist, her trim yellow rigging shining faintly, the water curling back from her sharp prow and yacht lines. The Swedish flag, a yellow cross on a blue field, was emblazoned on her sides and searchlights on her forward and aft decks were trained on her flags as she knifed up the Hudson to her Fifty-seventh Street pier.

"This was her first trip from her home port of Gothenberg across the North Atlantic. Her first voyage was made to South America when she was placed in service in January. She was built in 1940 and 'Lloyd's Register of Shipping' lists her as 411.6 feet in length and 53.3 in the beam. She is the first vessel to have left Sweden in the last two months.

"It was a perilous voyage, especially through the fog-shrouded, mine-laden waters off the Norwegian coast. She made her full sixteen knots, the better to get out of the way of such mines as were seen. Once she dodged five mines chained together. At night her master just trusted to the sea gods.

"Once the vessel was hailed by a British destroyer, which merely asked for her identification number. At various times both German and British bombing planes circled overhead. No attempt was made to stop or bomb her because she sailed with the joint consent of British and German admiralty officials.

"Passengers reported that '99 percent of Swedish citizens' are praying for a British victory despite German economic control of their country. The passengers told how Stockholm has become a 'hotbed of espionage' by German and British agents, and how Sweden is striving to build up her navy and is obtaining an average of one large and one small naval vessel a week.

"They said 200 to 500 German agents had been imprisoned since Christmas and several British agents had been arrested in the last few weeks. Motorbuses carry trailers with stoves for converting wood into charcoal to replace gasoline as fuel, and few merchant ships are able to get out.

"The passengers included the Misses Gurli Hallgren and Engrid Sillin (sic), who are coming here to be married; Professor Roman Jakobson, Russian exile who lectured on languages at the University of Upsala (sic), and Professor Ernst Cassirer, who will teach philosophy at Harvard University." [8]

During the course of the passage, Ingrid apparently grew to be very impressed by both the navigational skill and social exploits of the captain, a Swede by the name of O.E. Hultgren, so much so that she composed a poem that was almost as much about him as about her voyage. (What is it about men in uniform?!)

For vi lämnade Götet när som solen den steg opp,
Över bohusländska klippors gråa rand
"M/S *Remmaren*" var båten, svenska flaggan var i topp
Och på sidorna var blå och gula band.

Det var krig utivariden båd' till lands och uppå hav,
Mullret från kanon och bomb ljöd vida kring.
Nar vid Kreta och kring Lesbos gingo skepp och folk i kvav
Och vid Grönland dansa' flygare i ring.

Det var bistra tider när som *Remmaren* gick ut
For att bryta två blockaders hårda band
Men ombord fanns folk som visste hålla taget i en klut
Nar som stormen röt och sjön den bröt mot land.

Uppa bryggan stod kaptenen, O.E. Hultgren var hans namn,
Över alla oceaner var han känd.
Redan farfars far hans seglat, och hans far i varje hamn
Varlden runt hade en liten hjärtevän.

Själv han seglat haven runt från Berings Sund til Cape Good Hope,
Uppa brig och ångbåt, djonk och motorbåt,
Sidney, Singapore, Bombay, Valparaiso, Guadelope,
Säj den plats där han ej nån gång haft sin stråt.

Signoritor uti Spanien och töser i Hawaii,
Små japanskor, heta kvinnor i Peru,

American Bride

De fått leka med hans lockar, trycka tätt mot hans kavaj
Under heta karleksord, "How I love you."

Men O.E. Hultgren han har klarat varre stormar i sin dar
An den sköna kvinnor väckt uti hans bröst.
Och till landet långt dar borta, där en tös han lämnat kvar,
Styr han kosan då och då och finner tröst.

Men i stormen trivs han bäst och dundrar där till krigrts gud
Då kan intet hålle O.E.H. i land.
Då han brassar fulla klutar, styr mot oppna havet ut,
Och ger fan i både Tysk- och Engeland.

Blir han prejad av en ubåt för att tas till Hamburg in,
"Ich bin hier, und hier bleibt ich," då hörs hans hån,
Och om engelsmän försöka ta'n som pris till Aberdeen,
"Go to hell," det dundrar över havets dån.

M/S *Remmaren* den stävade mot Norges kala skar,
Sen åt väster, syd om Island kurs den tog,
Där var minor överallt, men de blott dansade isär
När kapten maskinsignalen på full fart slog.

Fyra, fem var bundna hop, men med en gir så elegant
Döden lurades på rovet denna gång.

Ifrån hytterna där nere lät det som en elefant
Snarkade, det var blott färdefolkets sång.
Och till New York vi kom fram efter fjorton lugna
dar
Uppå böljör som oss syntes oskuldsblå.
Enda faran som vi skådat – det var svårt för den
gå klar –
Var att inte spräcke tarmama i två.

Men mot Soderns länder styrde vår kapten sin
stolta båt,
Nya äventyr och karlatag emot.
Nya stormar skall han möta, höra nya flickors
gråt,
Möta nya minors och torpeders hot.

Men han är en äkta svensk och en sjutusan djäkla
karl
Som ej räds för faror eller själva fan.
Och fast kriget rullar på han säkert åter skutan tar
Till gamla Sverige, som är stolt över sin man.

My late cousin Stig Törnqvist sent Arne an attempt at an English translation after Ingrid's death. In an accompanying note he wrote, "I know that Ingrid was a great admirer of Evert Taube, our Swedish troubador, and I think that she had his song "Mote i Monsunen" ("Rendezvous in the Monsoon") in mind, because the text fits that melody perfectly. I enclose a copy of the melody (made on my computer, so it looks a bit funny). Ingrid's song reminds me a lot of Taube's narrative way of writing."

A War-time Voyage of the M/S Remmaren

I have used both Stig's translation and a more recent version by our cousin Carl-Erik Törnqvist as resources to render a rhyming version in English, with a consistent meter:

> We left Sweden in the morning, as the sun was coming up,
> Lighting up the naked rocks and islands, too.
> M/S *Remmaren*, our ship, the flag of Sweden up on top,

And its hull was striped with yellow paint and blue.

As the war was going on, both on the sea and on the ground,
And the rumbling from the guns and bombs was high.
Both down at Crete and around Lesbos ships and people going down,
While in Greenland fighter pilots filled the sky.

So the times were very trying as the *Remmaren* set out,
Seeking passage through the two blockading foes,
But its crew were able seamen who, without a doubt
Could 'midst raging seas and winds their will impose.

On the bridge stood O.E. Hultgren, the commander of the ship,
Throughout the world his name of great renown.
For his father sailed before him and did so his son equip,
Leaving girlfriends in 'most every port and town.

He had travel'd 'cross the oceans, Bering Sea to Cape Good Hope
On board brigs and steamers, junks and motorboats,
Sydney, Singapore, Bombay, Valparaiso, Guadeloupe,
He'd been ev'rywhere on anything that floats!

Señoritas down in Spain and Hawaiian lasses, too,

He left women in Japan and in Peru,
Who'd run fingers through his hair and plead him not to bid adieu,
While whisp'ring siren words, "How I love you!"

In many storms throughout his life has gallant Captain Hultgren fought
So much worse than pretty girls could cause his heart,
Yet a country far away holds one lass who draws his thoughts.
He returns to seek the comfort she'll impart.

He prefers the stormy weather and like Ares thunders he,
There is naught can keep him back upon the shore.
No, he charges full ahead, because his call is to the sea,
Though the British and the Germans are at war.

If a U-boat should confront him and command him into Kiel,
"Ich bin hier, und hier bleibt ich" he will cry.
If an English ship will take him as a prize, this man of steel,
"Go to hell," will bellow back as a reply.

M/S *Remmaren* she headed north 'long Norway's rocky coast,
Then westward, south of Iceland the ship sped.
Lots of sea mines ev'rywhere, but they parted like a ghost,
When the captain ordered "Give full speed ahead!"

Four or five were tied together, but with a turn so elegant,
He cheated death all night and we went free.
From the cabins came a noise, like a snoring elephant,
It was Hultgren's crew who sang so happily.

And so in New York we landed after fourteen pleasant days
On the sea, which looked so innocent and blue,
The sole risk that we had faced, and it was hard to keep away,
Was so much good food we almost burst in two!

And then Hultgren left New York for other missions of his trade,
Meeting challenges and hazards as he went,
Mast'ring threats from hostile shells and from torpedoes and grenades
Kissing other pretty girls with their consent.

He's all Swede, there is no doubt, for he is daring, he is smart,
He is scared of nothing, devils, go to hell!
Though the war is going on, more prudent courses he will chart
And proud Sweden his heroics will retell.

Without any reference to her poetry, Ingrid continued:

"We arrived in New York on June 4th. It rained heavily, and I could hardly see the Statue of Liberty. Arne was there waiting for me. The luggage had to go through customs. I had two trunks full of linen – sheets,

tablecloths and towels on which I had embroidered monograms. The customs officer asked if they had been used.

'Yes, of course,' Arne said. 'She has been sewing on them.' I also had a big rubber lifesaving suit.

'What's that?'

'A raincoat.' Arne said. 'You think this is rain, you should see it when it rains in Sweden!'

"Everybody chuckled, and he let me through."

Someone once said that three's a crowd, and Ingrid would likely concur. She was about to meet her first prospective in-law.

"We drove to Brooklyn, where Arne had a nice apartment on Shore Road. Anna Lisa was going to live nearby in Brooklyn, too, with her uncle and aunt. I was very happy to be able to lean on her. After we arrived, Arne's aunt from Chicago, Aunt Ruth, came as quickly as she could. She was to be our chaperone until we got married.

"It took some time to get ready for the wedding. We had to get certain papers in order, along with our blood tests. Aunt Ruth wanted to show me the American way of living, and I was not very impressed by that. She showed me several modern inventions in the kitchen, and I said, 'Oh, we had that in Sweden a long time ago!' I'm sure she was disgusted with me. I was not very nice to her.

Ruth Ragnvald (Aunt Ruth)

"One thing that really annoyed me was when she looked at my engagement ring. I was going to get a wedding ring that looked exactly the same. That's a Swedish custom.

"She said, 'That's very old-fashioned. Everybody here wears a diamond ring. When you have been married ten years, you are going to throw that away and get a diamond ring instead.'

"I told her that I thought a wedding ring was more important than that, and I liked the simple gold ring, because you can wear it whatever you do. If you have a diamond ring, when you scrub the floor or peel potatoes or do any dirty work, you have to take it off. And a wedding ring is supposed to be left on for the rest of your life. So there!

"Our wedding was held June 21, 1941 in Trinity Lutheran Church in Brooklyn, where Arne was a member. Pastor Scaer and Dr. Walter Maier of 'The Lutheran Hour' married us. The Scaers had been very helpful to arrange everything for the wedding. Their four-year-old daughter Jean was our flower girl. She was just adorable. Anna-Lisa and Florence Zimmermann [Mrs. Scaer's sister] were bridesmaids. Anna Lisa had a blue gown and yellow flowers. Florence had a yellow gown and blue flowers, Swedish colors. I had a rather simple long white gown and a long veil. I carried a Swedish bridal hymnal that my sisters and brothers had given me. It had long streamers of white ribbons with edelweiss flowers.

"It was extremely hot in church. People were fanning themselves with cardboard fans. Mr. Gustav Zimmermann, Mrs. Scaer's father, walked me up the aisle in my father's place. The organist played Scandinavian music for our benefit, but when he came to 'Finlandia,' the organ couldn't take it any more. It broke down, so he had to continue to play on the piano instead.

"I had learned to repeat after the minister, 'I, Ingrid, take thee, Arne, to be my wedded husband, etc.' I was very nervous and hardly knew any English, so I did not understand too much of Dr. Maier's talk. From church we went to the Hotel Bossert, where we had a very nice sit-down dinner for about thirty or forty people.[9] There were several speeches. I hardly understood anything, until the Norwegian Seamen's *pastor Gulbrandtsen came on. He had a very nice speech in Norwegian, and I was very thankful to him."*

Ingrid with her bridesmaids, Florence Zimmermann (on left) and Anna Lisa Montheli (right).

"Then they made me sing a Swedish song, 'Den första gång jag såg dig' ('The first time I saw you').

"None of our family were with us except for Torbjørn, who was stationed up in Toronto, Canada. [Note: Aunt Ruth was there, too!] He came down for the wedding, and we were happy to at least have him with us.

The wedding reception at the Hotel Bossert.

"We stayed overnight at Hotel Bossert. The following day we drove up to Pocono Pines and had a two-day honeymoon. Arne couldn't stay any longer, and he was on the phone with the office most of the time."

Ingrid had a rosier description of her honeymoon in a letter to her parents. Following is a translation made by my dear cousin, Ragne Moe:

Brooklyn, June 28th – July 1st 1941

Dear Dad and Mom,

I understand that you are anxious to hear about our wedding, and I have lots to tell if I only could sort it all out. Today we have been married for <u>a whole week!</u> I still haven't got quite used to it yet, and every time *somebody says Mrs. Pettersen I jump and think, "Is it me?"*

In the morning of June 21st we started the day with telephone calls, first from Norway and then from Sweden. It was all so touching, and we felt so grateful for all the thoughts and prayers from our dearest, both so far away and those who are close to us.

From you and my siblings there were telegrams, for which we warmly thank you. Arne's family were not allowed to telegraph and they and we felt bad about that. For a change Arne stayed at home that morning and we spent the day together until approximately 3 o'clock. Then Torbjørn took me to Anna-Lisa Montheli, my friend from the boat, and she helped me with the wedding dress. I had a long bridal veil, and instead of a bouquet I carried my Swedish hymnal with long white silk ribbons hanging down with small bouquets of white edelweiss. I held both that and my grandmother's bridal handkerchief in my hands. The ceremony should not start until 7 o'clock, so it was a day of waiting, but strangely enough I was not that nervous. I only felt an indescribable joy and happiness.

At 5 o'clock a car came and picked me and Anna-Lisa up and brought us to the Zimmermanns. They are Rev. Scaer's (from the church) parents in law. And Mr. Zimmermann should "give the bride away," i.e., stand in for the father of the bride. He is a lovable old man, well so is the whole family, and we have already become close friends even if I <u>unfortunately</u> don't cope with the English language yet. (But it is improving.)

From there we moved eventually to church where Arne – poor thing – already had been waiting for a while. First I was guided down to the basement, which was cool and lovely, but it seemed that the clock never would strike seven, and on top of that the organ broke down just as the ceremony was about to start. The poor organist was in despair, but there was a piano in the church – a quite good one, too – and it all ended well.

And by the music of Mendelssohn we walked slowly up the aisle – me by Mr. Zimmermann's arm and following us the little sweet bridesmaid Jean Scaer.

At the altar stood my beloved Arne waiting, and at that moment I saw <u>nobody else</u> except him. We were very pleased that Dr. Maier, who is a very busy man, had come to our wedding. The ceremony was officiated by Rev. Scaer – we had been practicing beforehand so nothing should go wrong.

I repeated: "I Ingrid, in the presence of God and this assembly take thee Arne, to be my wedded husband and plight thee my troth in every duty, not to part from thee till death us do part."

At this moment there were two hearts filled with joy and gratefulness. After the wedding ceremony Dr. Maier delivered a good message on Colossians 3.17. I hope he will write it down for us later.

The church was so beautifully decorated with flowers, it was so wonderfully solemn, and I was in such a blissful mood. You think you can't take so much joy and happiness. The church was crowded with people, both those who were invited and others that wanted to take part. We walked down the aisles to the tunes of Söderman's "Bröllopet på Ulvåsa" ("The Wedding at Ulvåsa"). Then all the people came and took our hands and congratulated us. (There are so many nice people in America I have found out.) Photographers followed us all the way from the church and throughout the party. I hope we can send you the photos later on.

<u>Continued, Tuesday, 1st of July</u>

Well, we went by cars to the Hotel Bossert for dinner. The atmosphere was the best thinkable, the food most excellent and the music – both Norwegian and Swedish – was so touching and beautiful, and when they played "Den fôrste gang jag såg dig" ("The First Time I Saw You") they made me stand up and sing it. It was crazy, but Arne whistled along and there I stood looking at him, my back turned to all the guests! What it sounded like, I don't know, but now it's done anyway. The evening was so terribly hot and we all sweated. It was all right for me in my light gown, but poor Arne was dressed in full evening dress, tailcoat, also called "father killer" and that made him hotter than before.

The table was beautifully decorated with flowers and candles and Swedish and Norwegian flags. There were many nice speeches and I understood quite a few. Dr. Maier had even a Swedish phrase, he wished "lycka hele livet igenom" (happiness ever after). I am so happy that I met him. I hope it is not the last time. About thirty guests participated at the dinner, everything went as well as it could be, but as you understand I was *thinking of you all back home and wished that you all could have been here on my happy day.*

Then eventually we withdrew without anyone knowing where to. Normally they would think on a honeymoon, but we stayed in a room in the hotel resting after an eventful day.

The day after we drove away from the heat and damp in New York and had a wonderful trip through a beautiful landscape and reached Lutherland in Pocono Pines in the evening. We stayed in a hotel for a few days. The reaction came afterwards. We slept and eased off, walked in the woods, went swimming and picked strawberries and felt like two happy children and forgot all about worries and sorrows.

The day came to break up and on Wednesday we started on our way home again. In the afternoon we were here again and were met by Aunt Ruth and another relative, May Pettersen. You should have seen all the presents that poured in. I hope it ends soon, because I don't know where to put all the stuff. The cupboards were pretty full already. A Japanese service for twenty-four persons that Arne had got takes much space, and we have got so much silver that will keep me busy for a long time polishing. But yesterday I packed lots of things in a suitcase as our apartment isn't that big to have all the things in view. Earlier it was almost like a jewelry store when all the gifts were on display! People must obviously have known my love for coffee, as we got four coffee services in silver and one in china. If there weren't a monogram on them we could have exchanged them for something else, but now we have to vary instead! And now we have to write thank you cards, personally and individually to each and everyone, and it seems that that would be my job. It is good anyway that one gets married only once in a lifetime.

Yes, now it seems that everything is in order and back to normal, well, that is Arne <u>absolutely</u> "has to" go to the office about 8 o'clock in the morning, but it has not been until 9 o'clock. When he has left, I do the housework, do the dishes and go shopping, etc. I have some difficulties in expressing myself, but when you laugh and look helpless, people are so helpful and nice, and now I have found out that I can phone to the grocery store to avoid going out in the heat. Arne comes home about 6 o'clock, sometimes earlier, sometimes later and then I have the dinner ready. I'm not a very good cook, but until now Arne has not complained and enjoys being home.

Yesterday I met Arne at the office and went with him and his colleagues to visit a ship, where we had a good time and enjoyed a nice meal on board. Last Sunday we went to the Norwegian Seamen's Church and later that day we went out in the country by the Hudson River and had a lovely day together.

The only thing that is hard to adjust to is the enormous heat. It sets you out and makes you unable to work. But out here where we live, we feel the breeze from the sea, and the temperature inside is not more than 30 degrees [86°F]. Outside it is about 40 degrees [104°F].

It is sad that this letter is delayed, but better late than never. As you understand everything is joy and happiness, and we feel luckier every day. Perhaps my siblings can take part in this letter, too.

All the best and warmest regards from
Arne and Ingrid

CHAPTER 9

A Swede in America

Beyond all these things put on love, which is the perfect bond of unity. Colossians 3:14

After returning from her honeymoon, and with Arne at work all day, Ingrid began to deal with the trials of being a newly landed immigrant in a foreign land. This was compounded by having to deal with a climate quite different from her native Sweden.

Newlyweds: Ingrid and Arne pose for Anna-Lisa in front of her uncle's home in Brooklyn.

"That summer in Brooklyn was very hot, and I was very homesick. I had had some English in school, but I was afraid to talk and make mistakes. But soon I noticed that people were used to foreigners, and they didn't laugh if you made any mistakes. I also noticed that natives of Brooklyn made mistakes. So I was brave and talked on, and I improved by and by.

"We took weekend trips out in the country, and I met many of Arne's Norwegian friends who lived in Bay Ridge. The captains from Fearnley and Eger ships always visited whenever they came to New York. I also had Anna Lisa nearby, and we got together quite often. I hadn't been in Brooklyn very long when I was going into Manhattan to meet Arne for lunch. He had explained exactly how to go on the subway, and I went. On the way, someone stopped me and asked for directions to a certain place. I had no idea, so I just pointed to a sign and said, 'Read the sign.'"

Just four months after her arrival in New York, Ingrid received a telegram from home. She wrote:

"In October 1941 we took a trip to Minnesota to attend the wedding of a second cousin of Arne's who lived in Evanston, Minnesota. That was my first time on an airplane, and it was exciting. When we came back from that trip, I was met by a telegram from Sweden. My mother had died. That was a very difficult time to get through."

With war raging in Europe, there was no way that she could go home and share her grief with the rest of the family. And the situation would only become worse. She continued her narrative:

"Then, on December 7, we had the attack on Pearl Harbor, and I knew I would have to stay for a while. At Christmas that year, Torbjørn came again, and we celebrated the holiday together. I wanted to go to a Swedish dawn service. We went to Gustavus Adolphus Church in New York at five o'clock in the morning, but it was so packed that we couldn't get in, so we went back to Brooklyn and attended a Norwegian church instead. We stayed in Brooklyn until the spring of 1942, when we moved to Crestwood. And that starts another chapter. You'll have to wait for that."

Chapter 10

Love and War

But now faith, hope and love abide these three; but the greatest of these is love. I Corinthians 13:13

After her account of December 1941, my mother never made another recording. She went home to be with her Lord on April 8, 1995, just a day before the fifty-fifth anniversary of her receipt of my father's proposal and two and a half months before what would have been their fifty-fourth wedding anniversary. That day also happened to be her father's birthday.

Many friends have found the duration of my parents' marriage quite remarkable, given the brevity of their courtship. But I am quick to remind them of my all-time favorite Chinese fortune cookie: "Love at first sight saves time and money!"

After my mother's funeral, which she herself had planned some ten years earlier, I discovered two leather-bound diaries in the attic of my parents' home in Rhinebeck, New York. They covered the period from my mother's twenty-sixth birthday on November 27, 1941 through the end of 1942 and were translated for me and my siblings by our beloved late cousin Stig Törnqvist.

One cannot help but be impressed by how quickly my mother adapted to such a dramatic change in her life – moving from the bucolic backwater town of Gesäter, Sweden to the fast-paced life as the wife of a rapidly rising young executive in New York. The thirteen months covered by her diary give insights into my parents' faith, the depth of their love for each other and the beginning of the sacrifices which the war was to force them to make.

Her diary begins with a reflection on her first birthday as a married woman:

> Thursday, November 27, 1941: *"The terrible alarm clock woke me up at 6 a.m. Arne sneaked out into the kitchen and after a while he came back with coffee and a lot of congratulations. And at that moment I realized that I had become one year older since yesterday! An old lady of 26! The coffee was good, and when that was finished I opened my packages. I got this nice book, almost too beautiful to write in. I got an enchanting Chinese teapot with a pack of tea, and an electric iron. I also got the receipt for my new winter coat which we ordered a week ago, and a lot of stationery with my initials. After breakfast Arne went to the office as usual. I looked in vain for a letter from Sweden. There must be something wrong with the mail. Then I walked to the hairdresser and got a shampoo. When I came back I found seven wonderful red roses with a card, 'From your friend.' About four o'clock I left for Arne's office to be there before five. We went to the Swedish restaurant 'Stockholm' and had a great dinner. Then we went to Radio City Music Hall, saw a movie and some performance. Back home at 11:30.*

Tired but happy with the day. I wish I could learn to be more grateful about everything."

Her next entries begin to describe Arne's and her efforts to preserve their traditions in observing Advent and celebrating Christmas. They also convey her frustrations with the increasing difficulty in communicating with her family back home, highlighted by the lack of any greetings of any kind on her birthday. The situation would only grow worse.

Sunday, November 30: *"Today is Advent Sunday. We went to the Scaers' church. Then we went back home and relaxed. Dinner at the Hotel Gregory. In the evening we lit our candles and sang Advent and Christmas hymns. We have a real Christmas atmosphere."*

Monday, December 1: *"Still no letter from Sweden! Patience, dear Ingrid! MS Vingaren is anchored just outside. Will probably go back to Sweden before Christmas. I got a bit homesick when I saw it. This afternoon I went to the office to meet Arne, and then we went to Kullan, a little Swedish store with imported Swedish things. We spent more than an hour, buying candlesticks, a bell tower and some other Christmas decorations. We had a walk on Fifth Avenue, looking at the extravagant Christmas window displays. It started raining, so we went some place to get a sandwich and a cup of tea. We picked up some Norwegian and Swedish records which we played in the evening."*

An entry in early December contains Ingrid's first reference to her pregnancy. If she was following her doctor's guidance, it appears to have been far less restrictive than that given by most obstetricians today, particularly with respect to diet, rest and alcohol consumption. With Arne leading his company, she was expected to attend a number of dinners with him as well as to entertain guests in their home quite frequently.

> Wednesday, December 3: *"Arne came home at five o'clock, picked me up and took me to Dr. Harris, where I was for the first time four weeks ago. My weight was 138 pounds. I paid $150. Have to go back there after three weeks. As usual, I didn't feel well in the car. It is no pleasure, either for Arne or me. We picked up Anna-Lisa on the way back. Played some new records for her, and then we played Chinese Checkers, of course."*
>
> Friday, December 5: *"Rain! I did a lot of shopping for the dinner tonight. Arne came home around six and the guests* [three couples] *arrived at seven. We had smörgåsbord, lamb steak, vegetables and dessert. They complimented me for the food, and I think it was a successful evening. The guests left at 11:00 p.m., and I was rather tired. The kitchen looks terrible. The dishes have to wait until tomorrow. They probably will not run away! Finally I got some letters from Sweden, one from Dad and one from Greta, dated November 14 and November 9, respectively."*

Ingrid's description of the attack on Pearl Harbor was very succinct, but the event was to set off a series of changes in their lives.

Sunday, December 7: *"Got coffee in bed. Then we went to the Swedish Seamen's church and listened to Rev. Thorbjörnsen. When we came home we heard that America is at war with Japan. Japan started the whole thing."*

Tuesday, December 9: *"To the dentist again! He never seems to be finished! Warning alarm! I didn't hear it, but it seems that many womenfolk are very nervous and upset, among them Mrs. Smith! I went to the office, sat there knitting. Then with Arne and Torbjørn to the Lexington Hotel where many Norwegians had gathered to form a new club, "A Liberated Norway." First dinner, then discussion until 11 p.m. We left before the end of the meeting. I got sick, so Arne had to stop the car so I could go out and do what was necessary. Ugh, Ingrid!"*

On Wednesday, December 10, Ingrid received a letter from her father, dated Nov. 17. In it he described the estate inventory proceedings to be held in Gesäter on December 17 and asked her to send a power of attorney to her brother Erik. She asked, "How shall I find time for that?"

Two days later Arne, the workaholic, felt so ill that he stayed home the whole day, plagued by headaches, vomiting and loss of appetite. Ingrid began to wonder whether there might be some problem with his stomach. However, he seemed to recover by the end of the day, so she continued with her plan to surprise him in the morning.

On Saturday, December 13, Ingrid quietly got out of bed, put on her wedding dress and awakened Arne at 6:30 with coffee, singing "Santa Lucia."[10] It appeared to have the desired effect, although she noted that he still seemed very tired. Nevertheless, he left for his office as usual. He returned at 4:30, his arms loaded with packages, greatly piquing her curiosity.

On Monday the 15th, Arne accompanied Ingrid to the Swedish Consulate to execute a power of attorney and send a cable to Sweden to confirm it. They then visited a Steinway piano store, after which Arne did some further research with his friend Captain Oddvar Blindheim. Ingrid was soon to learn the fruits of their effort.

> Wednesday, December 17: *"After a visit to the dentist I met Arne. We used Blindheim's car and went to look at a piano. Steinway, two years old, almost not used at all, wonderful sound. And Arne bought it! It will be delivered tomorrow. Wow! I am sure it is completely insane but very fun. Arne, the lovely boy, says that it is a late wedding gift. We paid $700. A new one is $1550. We celebrated the deal with a lobster dinner, my favorite food. Then we went to the cinema and saw some news. We split up at 6:30. Arne had to go to a dinner at the Astor Hotel, and I went back home. I washed tablecloths and curtains. Arne came back at 11:30, bringing a basket with five different wine bottles, a gift from someone. I had just finished wrapping*

Christmas gifts, and I have produced thirteen rhymes of varying quality!"

Thursday, December 18: *"Four gentlemen came at 7 p.m., delivering the grand piano. We had to move the big desk. I tried to play the piano, but it did not work out very well. I have to learn."*

Then, three days later, they found the occasion to mark another anniversary:

Sunday, December 21: *"We woke up early and remembered the DAY, six months ago. Arne gave me some packages with some records: Mendelssohn's 'Wedding March,' 'A Midsummer Dream,' Söderman's 'Wedding at Ulvåsa' and Grieg's 'Wedding March.' And some small lovely handkerchiefs with the following note, 'Do you remember the day six months ago, when you and I stood in front of the altar? This is to celebrate the wonderful time we have spent in the home you gave me. Your loving Arne.' And a little picture with an anchor, a cross and a heart, with the following verse: 'A three-part promise was once given to us, that Faith, Hope and Love will ever remain whatever the life will be. And Love will always come in the first place.' Oh, my dear beloved Arne! I wish I could show the depth of my love better. What have I done to deserve this happiness during these six months? And still I have the feeling that our love will increase day by day. Life is wonderful together with the one you love. I went up and gave all three of us coffee in bed. We played the wedding records and then we went to the Scaers' church, beautifully decorated with Christmas trees and tinsel. The new organ and the bell tower, donated by Arne, were used for the first time. They sounded great. After the service we went to the Scaers, delivering some gifts for the kids. We went for dinner at Borgholms restaurant on Long Island. With Rhein wine! In the evening we played and sang Christmas hymns."*

CHAPTER 11

First Christmas in America

"It seems that the Christmas message is more clear and comforting this year than ever before."

From Ingrid's diary, it is clear that Arne was doing everything he could to make his bride comfortable in her new surroundings. This included attending worship as often as possible in Swedish or Norwegian churches (where she could understand the language) and observing many of her native traditions. In view of the guidance given to pregnant women in America today, the reader may be surprised at the amount of partying that they did!

Tuesday, December 23: *"Lots of baking in the morning, preparation of Christmas ham, etc. I do hope that everything will be all right. Arne came back early, about 6 I think, with a lot of presents from business friends. Wine and whiskey, a big cigar box and a Christmas ham. Blindheim came along and borrowed a mattress for a friend who had come to visit him. When Torbjørn had arrived we went out in the rain and picked up a nice Christmas tree. And now it is here, smelling lovely and decorated with candles, flags, apples and tinsel. And tomorrow is Christmas Eve!"*

Christmas Eve, December 24: *"The day began with coffee in bed. After breakfast Arne went to the office as usual. I made arrangements for the lunch, planned to take place at 3 p.m. Anna-Lisa sent some beautiful flowers, and so did Captain Pettersen [no relation]. And yesterday I got flowers from the Blindheims, and I bought some myself the other day. So our beautiful home looks and smells like a garden! Poor Arne did not appear until four o'clock, loaded with more packages. I had set the table with a lot of decorations, and we had a good lunch with all traditional dishes. After the meal we had coffee and biscuits. The whole thing tasted good and Swedish. Even in America it is obviously possible to create a good Christmas atmosphere! We played Christmas records and relaxed. We were curious about all of the packages under the tree. Dinner at 7:30. Then we lit the Christmas lights, Arne read the Christmas Gospel, and I read a Christmas sermon by L. Hannes, which Dad always used to read at home. We played and sang. We have indeed very, very much to be grateful about. At most places around the world there is just war and chaos. It seems that the Christmas message is more clear and comforting this year than ever before. Then we started to open all of the presents. Torbjørn was the distributor. I have never before gotten so many things. Everything was from my dear husband. I got a collapsible umbrella, a wonderful case with perfume, an evening handbag, embroidered nightgowns, handkerchiefs, slippers, stationery, records, Norwegian tapestries and a work box. I cannot remember everything. Every gift had a rhyme. In the evening a bouquet with*

First Christmas in America

twelve marvelous roses arrived with a card, 'Your friend.' We went to bed at 12:30 a.m. We had planned to go to the early Christmas service at 4:30 at Gustav Adolf Church."

Christmas Day, December 25: *"The alarm clock rang at 3 in the morning. We closed our eyes again and woke up at 3:30! Now we were in a hurry. We rushed out, picking up Anna-Lisa, who waited for us. Arne drove fast, through red lights, etc., but the traffic was light and all policemen asleep. After getting lost a couple of times, we arrived at 4:30 and found out that the church was completely full. We were advised to wait until the next service, at 5:30, in English! What a disappointment! I was really sad. But we turned around and drove to the Bethlehem church at Pacific Street. They had a Swedish service at 5:30. We got our seats, and it was good to sing the well-known Christmas hymns in Swedish. All of us were a bit sleepy during the sermon. No wonder! Back home we all fell asleeep. At 9 o'clock Arne asked if I would like a cup of coffee. Ingrid said, 'NO THANKS!' and went on sleeping. Arne went back to bed, too, and we slept until 1 p.m. We had some 'breakfast' and then Arne and I took a nice long walk. All of the houses are so beautifully decorated! So this is my first Christmas in a foreign country. My thoughts have been with everyone at home. I am especially concerned about Dad, who is alone. And I miss receiving letters. But I have gotten cables with greetings, and I know that they are with me in spirit. First Christmas abroad, yes, but first of all the first Christmas in my own home together with my beloved Arne. I have so many things to be grateful about."*

Friday, December 26: *"The second day of Christmas is not a holiday in this country. I have many things to learn. We had planned to have dinner in the evening for the Norwegians at the office, some skippers who are in town and Anna-Lisa. About fourteen people. I was almost scared, more about the small space in our home than about the food. I went shopping early, and I had a lot of work to do the whole day. It takes longer to prepare food than to eat it! Arne and Torbjørn arrived at 6 p.m., and at seven the guests were coming. We started with smörgåsbord. We were eleven: the captains Paust, Gjörtz-Hansen, Andersen, Pallesen and Blindheim, Birger Gran, Björn Lie, Anna-Lisa, Torbjørn, Ingrid and Arne. Everyone had a good appetite and the atmosphere was the best. After dinner, Arne, Anna-Lisa and Blindheim went out to the kitchen to prepare glögg.[11] I had an old Swedish recipe which they tried to follow. But instead of measuring the spices in ounces, they measured in pounds! So the brew became a bit strong! We played a lot of games and really had a lot of fun. Coffee and fruit dessert. Nice guests, all of them, and I think they enjoyed the party. When they left, about 1 a.m., the kitchen was messy. I started to clean up, and poor Arne assisted me. In bed at 2:45 a.m."*

Saturday, December 27: *"Arne sneaked out of bed without my noticing, and he was almost dressed when I woke up. I got up and gave him some breakfast, then went to bed again and slept until 10:30. Torbjørn and I had breakfast, and then we cleaned the apartment together. Torbjørn is a great kid. Of course – he is Arne's brother! We had lunch when Arne came back at 2 p.m. Torbjørn took me to the hairdresser, and Arne picked me up. We went to a jewelry store and picked up a cute brooch for me to wear with my black dress. We went back home and dressed, Arne in his tuxedo, me in the long black dress, silver slippers and my new evening bag. Torbjørn wore his uniform. At 7 p.m. we arrived at the Zimmermanns. A lot of people had already come. It was so noisy that I almost got a headache. First cocktails, of course, then dinner with turkey and ham. We played a game which I did not understand. At midnight we went down to the basement and had beer! (We could better have had that with the food!) I was terribly tired, so we left before the rest of the company. Torbjørn stayed, so we got a lift with someone else. In bed at 2. In my opinion, people eat too much and sleep too little at Christmas time!"*

Sunday, December 28: *"We were sleepy in the morning. Arne brought me coffee in bed. After breakfast we went to the Norwegian Seamen's Church and listened to Rev. Manne, who has been a missionary in India. I was sleepy, and the pastor did nothing to improve the situation. The most sleepy performance I have ever heard! We said hello to him after the service and asked him to our home on Saturday, Jan. 2. I will try to invite [some other*

Norwegian couples] to come at the same time. After church I took a nap and the boys played chess."

Monday, December 29: *"At 4 p.m. I took the subway to the office. Arne had gotten a basket full of grapefruit from Texas. They were red inside. Wow! We went to Dr. Harris. I have gained 3 pounds since the last visit. Got some medicine for my leg. I have to come back in three weeks. When we came back home I felt very lousy and vomited. After tea, Arne took Torbjørn to the airport. He had to go back to Toronto. We will miss him. He will probably come back in June. I went to bed at 7:30 and slept until about 10, when Arne woke me up with five red roses!"*

Wednesday, December 31: *"New Year's Eve! Poor Arne did not feel well. He stayed home from the office and in bed the whole morning. Luckily he recovered in the afternoon, so we could go to the late service at the Seamen's Church. It was a wonderful service. Rev. Gulbransen preached. Afterwards he came with us back home. So, another year is finished. We think of so many events, happy and sad, during the last year, but I have far more reason to be grateful than to complain. During the past year I have experienced the happiest day of my life – when I married my dear husband. I hope that our mutual happiness will remain and grow even stronger during the years to come. And may we be able to thank God for his grace to us."*

Chapter 12

A New Year

"No one can be happier than I, and I am convinced that nobody has a husband like Arne."

The entertaining continued in the New Year, often in the company of the clergy, including the Revs. Gulbransen, Manne, Thorbjörnsen and their wives.

Friday, January 2: "I worked hard the whole morning to prepare for the party in the evening. Arne came about 6 p.m. and the guests arrived about seven.... Smörgåsbord with various Christmas food, and strawberries for dessert. A good atmosphere, nice people, especially Rev. Thorbjörnsen and his cute wife. I hope I will get to know them better. We sang a lot of songs and Rev. Manne played. We played some games and the guests left about midnight. I was tired and happy."

During this time, Arne continued to meet regularly with the "Liberated Norway" group, typically not arriving home until well after midnight.

With the prospect of their first child, anticipated some time in June, Arne and Ingrid decided that they would need larger living quarters. Arne contacted his close friend Fred Nehring, a successful realtor who lived with his wife Helene and family in Westchester County, just north of Manhattan. It didn't take them long to decide on their new home. Ingrid described their initial foray into the suburbs:

> Saturday, January 10: *"We got up early and left at 8:30 to meet Mr. Nehring in New York and look at some houses in the countryside. His son came with us in our car to their home, where Mrs. Nehring served wonderful coffee. After that an older woman took care of us and showed us some more or less nice houses. There was one house, opposite the Nehrings, a huge one with ten rooms, but a shabby bathroom and kitchen. No garage. I decided right away that I do not want to live there! We saw some other places, not too interesting. The monthly rent for the houses was an average of $75, and they were too big. Then we came to a small house, and I fell in love with it immediately. We have almost decided to go for it. The address is 211 Scarsdale Road, Crestwood, New York. The house is built in an old English style, with a chimney outside one of the walls. A large Christmas tree stands at one of the corners. And a small garden framed by a stone wall and a pond with a murmuring creek and a little bridge. In the basement there is a garage, laundry room and storage. On the first floor there is a living room with a fireplace and a porch for the lady's flowers. A nice kitchen in green and beige, very roomy. On the second floor are three rooms: one master bedroom, one guest room and a library, where Arne can devote himself to his beloved books. The bathroom is charming, and there is one additional shower room. When we had looked at all of this for a couple of hours, we returned to the*

Nehrings for lunch. Then we went home, planning, dreaming and decorating 'our' house in spirit."

211 Scarsdale Road, Crestwood, New York

The following day was Arne's thirty-first birthday, and Ingrid seemed intent on making it a memorable occasion. Her diary entry included an episode that might have played well on "I Love Lucy," a television show that became one of their favorites a decade or so later.

> Sunday, January 11: *"Arne's birthday! Coffee in bed and singing with my husky morning voice. At 8 o'clock two 'singing telegrams' arrived, one over the phone and one delivered by three guys with no singing voice. I gave Arne a wallet, a magnifying glass, a scarf and red roses. I think it was appreciated. At least the dear boy said that this was his best birthday ever. After breakfast we drove to*

the Seamen's Church where we listened to Rev. Thorbjörnsen. Then we went for lunch to Lundins. I had decided to make ice cream for the party tomorrow. And when the mixture was whipped it had to be stirred over boiling water. The bowl cracked into thousands of pieces, and the great mixture with 8 eggs was mixed with the water! I became so upset that I both cried and laughed. Arne tried to comfort me, but when I started making a new mixture I discovered that there was no milk left. Arne had just put the car in the garage, but he took it out and went to the store and picked up milk and eggs. That lovely boy! And the ice cream turned out to be a success."

Monday, January 12: *"Cleaning, setting the table, cooking. I didn't know how many guests to expect, so I set a big table. I went to the butcher and picked up some beef. And then I spent some busy hours, exhausting but fun. Arne came home about 5:30 and did not feel well so I pushed him into bed to relax until the guests were to arrive. Poor Arne. There must be something wrong. Anna-Lisa came first, then the rest: Halstensens, Thorbjörnsens, Gustavsens, Blindheim, Gran, Bjørn and Captain Paust. The party was a success and the ice cream was fine, with pineapple and chocolate sauce. We had a really good time."*

The following evening, Arne returned home with a signed rental contract for the house in Crestwood. After entertaining more dinner guests on the 14th, Ingrid and Arne began packing the following day. They brought a lot of boxes and bags out to their car, and, with obvious excitement, Ingrid noted in her diary, "Tomorrow we will go to our 'new' house!"

> Friday, January 16: *"I picked up Arne at the office around 12. After a quick lunch we took off for the house, arriving around 1:30. We got the keys from Mrs. Logan, along with some wallpaper samples. She told us that some water pipes had frozen, but that they would be fixed shortly. Inside the house it was a bit cold, and the plumbers had made a real mess. Pity, it looked so nice during our first visit. We took a lot of measurements in all of the rooms. After that we were tired and a bit cold. So we went to the Nehrings, who served us dinner. We had to leave right after dinner, because Arne was supposed to attend another meeting of the Liberated Norway group."*

On Sunday the 18th, after worshiping at the Norwegian Seamen's Church in the morning, they went to the Scaers' church in the afternoon for a special service at which the new organ was dedicated. Ingrid continued packing for the next two days, only taking out time for a scheduled visit with her obstetrician, Dr. Harris, on Monday evening. Then another anniversary celebration!

> Wednesday, January 21: *"Today we have been married for 7 months! Time is passing quickly! I picked up Arne at 5 p.m., and then we were lucky enough to get tickets to Sonja Henie's skating show at Madison Square Garden. We had a couple of hours free, so we went to a news cinema, then for dinner at the Stockholm restaurant. In my opinion,*

the skating show was extraordinary. And little Sonia is so cute."

Over the next week, Ingrid and Arne found time for dinners with several of their friends in the midst of packing, an occasional side trip to Crestwood with more of their things and, of course, Arne's increasing demands at his office. Then, for Ingrid at least, moving day arrived.

Thursday, January 29: *"I went with Arne in the morning to say goodbye to Brooklyn. Arne went with me on the subway to Grand Central Station, from where I took a train to Tuckahoe. I arrived at 10:30, did some food shopping and took a taxi to the house. The wallpaperers were not yet finished with the guest room. It will take another day. I washed the windows and did a lot of other work. A new ice box arrived, a fancy machine called 'Norge.' It is now installed. Nice weather, sun and snow. At 7 p.m., Arne came with Blindheim and Gran, bringing some remaining small stuff from the apartment. We had coffee and sandwiches, and they all left about 9:00. And tonight I will sleep alone in a house furnished with only one bed. Arne called when he got home. How sweet of him!"*

Friday, January 30: *"Last night I was alone, the first time since we got married. And it is a long time since my sleep was so interrupted. I heard a lot of strange noises all the time. At last morning arrived, and I got up. The wallpaper people came around 8. I went to Tuckahoe to find out about the local shopping facilities. Seems OK. I bought some* fish. *Arne arrived around lunch time. It was a lovely reunion after a long, lonely night! About 2 o'clock the moving van arrived, and again we had to face a mess. When we were alone again we started sorting things, working hard until late."*

On February 1, their first Sunday in Crestwood, Ingrid and Arne went to church at Concordia, a Lutheran school in Bronxville about two miles from their new home. Afterward, they donned some ski wear and drove to an area called Salisbury Mills, where some Norwegians were having a skiing competition. Ingrid recalled that they stood in a freezing rain for about an hour, then had dinner at a small Italian restaurant on the way home. The following evening, after she had prepared dinner, she began knitting while waiting for Arne. When he arrived, his appearance alarmed her.

Monday, February 2: *"He came around 7, in a very bad condition. He vomited the whole night. Poor boy. I feel so worried. I don't know what to do, and there is nobody I can ask. The worst thing is that Arne is aware of my anxiety. I cannot control myself, and I think that I am a very poor nurse for my husband. Anyway, tomorrow he has to see the doctor."*

Tuesday, February 3: *"Arne slept well, but he was tired and faint when he woke up. He left for the office later than usual, but he insisted on going there! He came back around 8:30 p.m. He had seen the doctor, who gave him the same medicine as last time. But I would recommend a thorough examination of his stomach."*

For the rest of the week, Arne apparently commuted to and from New York without incident. When he was back in Crestwood, he and Ingrid kept busy shopping and furnishing their home. Although she had already commented a number of times about the friendliness of the Americans she encountered, Ingrid recalled one instance in particular:

> Monday, February 9: *"In the afternoon I went to Tuckahoe to take the train to New York. When I got the ticket, I discovered that I had left my money at home, so I couldn't pay! I didn't have a single penny! The next train was scheduled an hour later. I was so unhappy. But I summoned a lot of courage and asked the man in the ticket booth if I could come back tomorrow and pay. He was very understanding, and he agreed. And I asked if I could get another five cents for the subway! And he agreed to that as well. Lucky me! Around five I arrived at Arne's office. He didn't feel well, but he was not as bad as last week. We went to Dr. Harris, who listened to my stomach and declared that either I had a baby inside or I had swallowed a clock! I was so happy that he heard something. I had been a bit worried about the absence of movement, though I had now passed halfway through my pregnancy. He said that everything was OK, and I hope that I can trust him."*

Several days later, Ingrid got her own confirmation of what Dr. Harris had told her.

> Thursday, February 12: *"Lincoln's birthday. Arne was at home the whole day! We have installed the*

new furniture in the bedroom and moved the old things up to the attic. We went to Tuckahoe and bought a lot of plants for $9.50. The florist was so excited that I got two extra pink roses! Yesterday, I felt very clearly that something was moving in my stomach! I am so happy. Arne seemed to be happy, too, when I told him. It has been so nice to have Arne at home the whole day. I wish it could be a holiday more often!"

A week later, on February 19, Ingrid got some upsetting news. She wrote, *"I saw today in 'Nordstjernan'* [literally, Northern Star, a Swedish newspaper] *that Capt. Hultgren on the M/S 'Remmaren' had died in Buenos Aires. He was so cheerful, respected and loved both by passengers and crew."* She had nearly idolized him in her poem about her voyage to America. After the United States entry into the war, Swedish merchant traffic was denied access, and Argentina had assumed greater importance as a trading partner.

On Sunday, February 22, Arne and Ingrid attended a small church, Trinity Lutheran, in the neighboring town of Scarsdale for the first time and met its pastor, Rev. Emil Luecke. It was not long before it became their new church home. The following day was a holiday because of Washington's birthday. To Ingrid's growing consternation, Arne was not feeling well, and she remarked that he stayed home the whole day. They lit a fire in the fireplace in the evening and listened to President Roosevelt. The following day, Arne went back to work, but he exhibited increasing signs of stress and had difficulty sleeping. This was compounded by both Arne's and Ingrid's concern about their families back home, particularly in light of the near shutdown in communications.

On February 24, they received a telegram from Ingrid's brother Erik reporting that there had been no bomb damage at the University in Oslo, where Arne's father Stefanus worked. Erik went on to say that the last letter they had received from America was Ingrid's Christmas letter and that they hadn't gotten any letters from Norway since mid-December. In her diary entry that day, Ingrid wrote:

> "I think the whole situation is gloomy. There is no point in writing when the letters don't reach anyone. From Norway we can obviously get no sign of life, and from Sweden only telegrams. The last letter we got from Sweden was dated November 27 [her birthday]. In that one, we learned that Arne's father is very ill. He had gotten angina pectoris and was expected to stay in the hospital for about six weeks. After that we heard nothing. I am sorry for Arne. He doesn't talk much about it, but I understand that he is worried."

The pace of their busy lives may have been a blessing, helping to keep them from dwelling too much on the problems back home. In addition to working long hours at his office, Arne continued to meet with the Liberated Norway group, resulting in even later nights now that they lived in the suburbs. On February 28, they traveled to Philadelphia for a wedding. On March 4 Arne attended a dinner at the Waldorf Astoria, for Crown Prince Olav and his wife, now living in exile with the rest of the Norwegian royal family in London. He didn't get home until 2:30 in the morning, yet still went back to the office for a day of work before he and Ingrid attended another event for the royal couple at the Hotel Biltmore the next evening. Ingrid was duly impressed. She wrote:

> "At 8 o'clock we went up to the big hall. Almost 300 people were there. It was a magnificent dinner hall. A big table for the Crown Prince Couple and the Board and lots of smaller tables around. Beautiful music by 'Bergensfjords' orchestra. The Crown Prince made a beautiful speech, toasts to King and President. The Norwegian and U.S. flags were hoisted, and both countries' anthems were sung. The Crown Princess was so cute, but she had aged a lot. After dinner all of the guests walked in a procession, were introduced and shook hands with the royal couple. Then there was a concert. It was over about 11:30. I am so glad that I came along. It was a real experience."

The euphoria did not last long. On Tuesday, March 10, Ingrid received a telegram from her brother Erik, informing them that Arne's father had died two days earlier. Now, less than nine months into their marriage, they had each lost a parent, and they were unable to attend the funeral for either of them. It was also virtually impossible even to send any kind of message of condolence to the family in Norway. She wrote:

> "It was probably expected, but it is hard to deal with anyway. After some consideration, I called Arne and told him. He reacted very quietly. I am more worried about Torbjørn. Arne will send him a

telegram. I went to Tuckahoe and bought some roses for my Arne. Arne did not attend the planned dinner. He came home early. I am very concerned about Arne's mother. I cannot even write her a letter."

As she entered her final trimester, Ingrid focused more and more on her baby, convinced that it was going to be a boy.

Monday, March 23: "I went to New York in the afternoon, picked up Arne at the office, and we went to Wanamaker's and bought a nice big blue coat for me. I can use it also when I become slim again. Then we looked at baby beds, and we finally found one, a nice birch bed with painted pictures. It was designed in a clever way so that it can also be used when the baby is up to five years old. It came with a mattress, and we paid $34.95. Children are expensive! Then we saw the doctor, everything OK. He is very satisfied with me! My weight is 151 pounds. If I continue like that, gaining one pound a week, I will end up like an elephant!"

On Wednesday Arne left for a three-day business trip to Washington, D.C., and Ingrid saw him off at the station. It was the longest they had been separated since her arrival in the U.S. With pleasant early spring weather, she busied herself with gardening and cleaning up the yard. Anna-Lisa came to stay overnight the first evening to keep her company. At the end of the week, she was greeted by a flood of mail from home.

A New Year

Friday, March 27: *"I had a surprisingly good night's sleep. When I went downstairs to make breakfast, I had to open the door for the mailman who brought no fewer than eleven letters from Norway and Sweden! I was surprised and glad. I was busy for a couple of hours reading them all. There was one letter from Arne's father, written on December 16 when he was in the hospital. He looked forward to coming home around New Year's, but he seemed to be comfortable with his situation. I felt so melancholy when I read that letter, but at the same time I was glad to receive it. It was like a special goodbye. Then there was a letter from Astri, three postcards from Dad, mailed in January, two letters from Greta, one from Anna, one from Erik, one from Ella and one from Thea. I was glad to get so many letters. Poor Dad had been sick and away from work the whole month of December. He celebrated Christmas in Göteborg with Greta, Bertil and the children."*

As she thought about her father, it was painful to imagine how difficult things must have been for him, just newly widowed and absent from the pulpit he had occupied for more than forty years.

Two days later, on Palm Sunday, Ingrid was expecting three guests for dinner – Anna-Lisa and Captain and Mrs. Blindheim. But they arrived with a fourth -- the Blindheims' dog, Tösa, who had sailed with the Captain on his last ship. Ingrid and Arne had discussed getting a dog, but the timing of this gift came as a bit of a surprise. However, Tösa endeared herself to Ingrid quickly. They became almost constant companions, and caring for her new pet may have helped prepare for the anticipated arrival in June.

Several days after Easter, it was time to celebrate yet another anniversary.

> Thursday, April 9: "When Arne came home he brought a big bunch of flowers. Two years ago today I received the first letter from Arne. And that must be celebrated. It is also exactly two years since Norway was occupied, so there are a lot of Norwegian programs on the radio."

Three days later, on Sunday, April 12, Ingrid and Arne traveled by train to Baltimore for the christening by Crown Princess Märtha of an American hospital ship[12] named *St. Olaf*. The festivities were also attended by Crown Prince Olav and Wilhelm Morgenstierne, Norway's foreign minister in Washington.

After attending church on Sunday, April 19, Arne and Ingrid celebrated their ten-month anniversary two days early with a lobster dinner at a local restaurant. On Monday, when Arne came home from work, he was experiencing acute stomach pains and could not eat any dinner. Although he seemed to recover later in the evening, he had a recurrence just eleven days later, with pain severe enough that he came home early from the office. Despite these attacks, he continued to take every opportunity to expose Ingrid to the wonders of her new country. On one such occasion, after work, he took her to see her first circus. She was very impressed and excited by the performance and all of the "strange animals."

A New Year

By early May, the impact of the war started hitting home. Ingrid registered for a sugar ration card on May 6th, and ten days later Arne registered for their gasoline ration, just three gallons a week. Blackouts increased in both frequency and duration. Arne also registered for possible military service, while the work demands at his office continued to increase. Even on Saturday, he didn't come home until eight o'clock in the evening, and it didn't appear that he would be able to take any time off in the summer. His stomach attacks increased in frequency. Ingrid became concerned that he was working himself to death. On May 21, the celebration of their eleven-month anniversary was limited to a "nice walk in the evening."

On June 1, Ingrid was presented with a unique opportunity to improve mail delivery to her family. She took the train into New York that day to see her obstetrician, Dr. Harris. After her appointment, she and Arne went to the train station to meet a man by the name of Folke Littnin, who had arrived the previous day on a ship from Lisbon and had contacted Arne. He had brought some letters for Ingrid from her family.

Ingrid then realized that Folke had been a patient of hers at Sahlgrenske Hospital in Göteborg several years before. They took him to dinner and a movie, after which he agreed to take some letters from Ingrid and mail them upon his return to Lisbon. She spent the following morning writing furiously, with letters for each of her siblings and one for her father, in which she enclosed a number of photographs. She went back to Arne's office that afternoon. They reconnected with Folke, and he took her letters with a promise to mail them when he got back to Portugal.

On June 4, it was time for another celebration – the first anniversary of Ingrid's arrival on the *Remmaren*. She wrote:

> "What a lot of things I have experienced during this year! I have so many things to be grateful about. No one can be happier than I, and I am convinced that nobody has a husband like Arne."

She served Arne coffee in bed and then planned a dinner to include three of her fellow travelers, Anna Lisa and the Svensons. She set a beautiful dinner table, adorned with roses and jasmines, and afterward they enjoyed a relaxing evening together. Five days later she commented:

> Tuesday, June 9: "My little boy, due to scientific calculations, is programmed to be delivered today. But I think the calculations are wrong."

Nevertheless, she made up the crib and packed a bag, ready to leave on a moment's notice. With each passing day, she grew less patient and more uncomfortable. Persistent inquiries from her neighbors as to her status didn't help. Arne was becoming more uncomfortable as well, with recurring stomach pain, particularly after attending obligatory dinners that seemed to be a regular part of his responsibilities.

CHAPTER 13

A New Life

Whenever a woman is in travail she has sorrow, because her hour has come; but when she gives birth to the child, she remembers the anguish no more, for joy that a child has been born into the world. John 16:21

On Friday the 19th, Ingrid went in to New York to see her obstetrician, Dr. Harris, who suggested that she take a couple of ounces of castor oil to speed things up. She and Arne bought the oil on their way home, had tea on their veranda and fell asleep. Two days later, she wrote her longest diary entry by far, detailing the events of both the 20th and 21st. (The reader may note some changes which have taken place in the practice of obstetrics over the past seventy years!)

[On the 20th] *"I woke up at 1:30 in the morning and felt a bit strange. I had pains throughout my whole body, coming in waves every fifteen minutes. I guessed what was going to happen. I got up and got ready to leave. Poor Arne also woke up, shaved and put on his new suit, ready to become a father. I packed, made the beds, cleaned up the kitchen and had a shower. We locked Tösa in the basement, and Arne wrote a note for Mrs. Smith and attached a key. We put that at her front door. We left at 3:45. The trip went OK, but I had my pains every 15 minutes. We reached the hospital at 4:45, and a nice nurse took care of us. She took me in a wheelchair in the elevator, and Arne followed with my luggage. Then I had to say goodbye to Arne, and I was taken into an examination room. Got undressed and got a white shirt and white stockings. They placed me on a table, and then the whole thing began. Cross examination about my name, age, height, etc. It hurt when they pushed my stomach. I cried.*

"*They said, 'Don't cry!'*

'*That's easy for you to say,' I said.*

"*Then they took me into an adjacent room, the delivery room, and they left me on the table, fighting with my pain. At seven a nice elderly nurse came into the room. She turned out to be Norwegian. She put me in a chair, where I had to wait. After a while I climbed onto the bed when the pain increased. Then a female doctor came, squeezed my poor stomach and said it would take some more time. Not the least bit comforting! There I was, feeling abandoned, trying not to cry. And I didn't know where Arne was. He probably was dealing with his own torment, and I knew that he was thinking of me. At 8 I got some breakfast. Then the frequency of the pains increased, one peak every other minute. So at 9 a nurse took me back into the delivery room. I thought I could tear my hair out – the torment was indescribable. However, every mother has to go through this to get her little darling. At 10 a.m. Dr. Harris came to see me. He is great! About 11 o'clock I got laughing gas, a blessed invention. And from somewhere far away I heard somebody say that the baby had blond hair! I woke up at 11:20, listening to the sound of a child! And I felt that my stomach was gone! The sound came from my baby! It is impossible to describe how happy I was. I laughed and cried at the same time. It was a little girl with blond hair and blue eyes. And she is as welcome as a boy. And I don't think that Arne is disappointed. I was taken to my room about noon. It was lovely to stretch out in the bed. Arne came about 1 p.m., bringing seven red roses. It was lovely to hug him again. I think he was as happy as I am. He stayed for a couple of hours, and we phoned the Bendixens and Zimmermanns to tell them the good news. Arne went to send telegrams to Sweden and Norway. He came back about 8 o'clock and stayed an hour. He's gotten a room at the St. George Hotel. Then I got a visit from my little daughter, who wanted me to feed her. She had a good appetite, and she stayed with me almost an hour. She is so cute. Then Dr. Harris came to see me. Today is June 21, our wedding day! I feel fine, though I'm aching all over. I have gotten so many beautiful flowers from all of our friends. Anna-Lisa came to see me, and she brought flowers, too. Nice to see her again. Then Arne came back after having lunch with the Zimmermanns. Anna-Lisa promised to take all the blue baby clothes back to the store and get pink ones instead. Arne has met his daughter today. We cannot agree which of us she resembles! We have decided her name: Alice Birgitta. I was quite sure that I wanted to give her my mother's name. Arne is not allowed to be in my room when I feed the baby! He left in the evening to see that everything is OK at home. It was so nice to have him here for such a long time today. Now I know, more than ever, that I am the happiest person in the world."*

Friends continued to send congratulatory messages, along with gifts for little Alice. Ingrid wrote, *"It is much more pleasant to get things for my daughter than flowers for me."*

"Uncle" Torbjørn sent a telegram from Toronto. Aunt Ruth wrote in a letter, "Your little girl will be beautiful like her mother and intelligent like her father." Ingrid remarked, "From that one can draw the conclusion that Arne is not beautiful and I am not intelligent!" She fretted that she had heard nothing from her family in Sweden, but a telegram finally arrived on the 25th, assuring her that they had received the good news.

On June 27, still in the hospital, Ingrid wrote, *"Today Alice is one week old. It is hard to understand that such a small creature can take such a lot of room in my heart."*

Arne came in the afternoon, bearing a letter from Torbjørn and seven more red roses, one for each day of his daughter's life. On June 29, Ingrid was finally allowed to get out of bed and walk around for the first time. (How times have changed!) She looked in a mirror and admired her restored slim shape. She and little Alice were finally discharged and went home on Wednesday, July 1. Preparations were already well underway for Alice's baptism four days later, and Torbjørn came down from Toronto to spend his final days of leave with them. They had asked the Zimmermanns to be Alice's Godparents.

So on the fifth of July, Arne, Ingrid and Torbjørn drove back to Brooklyn with Alice, where she was baptized in Trinity Lutheran Church by Pastor Paul Scaer. Ingrid couldn't keep from crying as she realized it was her baby who was to be christened. She prayed that the Lord would give her and Arne the strength and wisdom to become good parents.

After the service, the baptismal party returned to Westchester, first for coffee at home and then for dinner at Schmidt's Farm, a restaurant in Scarsdale that had apparently become their favorite local eatery. Ingrid remarked that the table had been set beautifully, with lots of flowers, but that it was obvious that Arne wasn't feeling well.

Three days later, on Wednesday, Folke Littnin came for a visit, prior to his planned return to Sweden on the MS *Drottningholm*. Ingrid seized the opportunity to entrust him with some pictures for her family, including some from Alice's baptism. Torbjørn left the next day. Having now completed his studies at 'Little Norway' near Toronto, he was commissioned as a lieutenant in the Norwegian Air Force and had received orders to his first assignment -- in Iceland.

CHAPTER 14

"In Sickness and in Health"

"I Ingrid, in the presence of God and this assembly, take thee Arne, to be my wedded husband and plight thee my troth in every duty, not to part from thee till death us do part."

On Monday, July 13, Arne did not get home until 9:30 p.m. He was too weak to walk from the station, so he took a taxi. He was very pale, and Ingrid was scared. On Tuesday morning he was still weak and had difficulty getting out of bed. He went to the office, but only after promising Ingrid that he would see a doctor. He called her in the afternoon from Grand Central Station to let her know the diagnosis – a bleeding gastric ulcer – and that he was being sent directly to White Plains Hospital, about six miles and two railroad stops north of their home in Crestwood. He was not allowed to stop at home on the way.

Ingrid was heartbroken. Her responsibilities with Alice prevented her from going to see him immediately. But after a feeding she entrusted her with one close friend and neighbor while another drove her to the hospital.

Arne was so thin and pale that she burst into tears, but that seemed to release some of her tension. She realized that he was getting the care he needed, including being put on a strict diet. Ingrid found a way to visit him every day, often remarking how friendly and helpful her neighbors were, both in agreeing to care for Alice and in occasionally offering her rides to the hospital so that she didn't have to take the long walk if she went by train. Anna-Lisa came to help out on weekends.

It wasn't until July 27, two weeks after Arne's admission to the hospital, that the doctors felt comfortable that the bleeding had stopped. That same day it rained heavily, and Ingrid experienced for the first time how that charming murmuring stream behind their house had gotten its name – Troublesome Brook! The basement flooded, and her entire garden was under water. She had to deal with it herself, and she felt very lonely.

As a busy young mother with her husband in the hospital, Ingrid wrote less frequently in her diary, but her entries were filled with emotion. Yet, by the end of July she had filled all of the pages in the book Arne had given her on her birthday. In anticipation of that, he had ordered a new one. Her first entry in it was on Friday, July 31:

> "I got this beautiful book this morning from Georg Jensen [a specialty store], ordered by my dear Arne. This book is green – the color of hope. I hope that I will get my dear Arne back home soon. He is still at White Plains Hospital, fortunately better now. The last few days he has been able to sit in a chair for a couple of hours, and that is progress. But that is also an exercise to make him fit enough for a new X-ray on Monday. He has now been in the hospital for nearly three weeks, so I think it is time for him to come home soon to me and Alice."

She was cheered up that day by a telegram from Torbjørn, "from the other side," reporting that all was well with him. It had been fourteen days since he had left Toronto, and this was the first she had heard from him. She also received a letter from her sister Anna, mailed on July 2, and was encouraged that mail deliveries might be returning to a near normal schedule. That proved not to be the case, however.

On Wednesday, August 5, Ingrid and a neighbor drove to the hospital to finally bring Arne home. He had been there for twenty-two days. He was still tired and very weak but began to show improvement day by day. He remained on a very strict diet. Ingrid remarked how that made it easy for her, since she bought baby food for both him and Alice! During his time at home, he and Ingrid delighted in the rapid growth and development of their daughter. But the Sunday after Arne came home, it began to rain heavily. The storm continued for two days, and Troublesome Brook again lived up to its name. Ingrid wrote, *"The creek in the garden turned into a river, and behind the house the garden became a lake, flowing into the garage. Not as much as last time, but enough for us to decide not to buy this house."*

Arne enjoyed the luxury of time to play with and get to know his daughter. He didn't even mind changing her diapers. By the beginning of September his hemoglobin level had improved enough for his doctor to suggest that he might be able to go back to work in two weeks, and he drove the car for the first time since his hospitalization. The addition of Alice to their family allowed them to get another sugar ration card. In less than three months she had more than doubled her birth weight, from slightly less than seven pounds to more than fourteen. Ingrid remarked that she "is growing wildly" and that "she eats like a horse! She will become a female giant!"

Arne was finally cleared to go back to his office on Monday, September 28, after an absence of more than two and a half months. He began to ease back into his former routine -- that is, except for his diet. In early October, he and Ingrid were invited for dinner aboard a ship that had docked in New York. The entree was grouse, which had been shot by the captain in Greenland. Arne watched everyone else feast on it while he had a bowl of diet soup. It was the first evening that Ingrid had been away from Alice. When they came home that evening, they found her sleeping contentedly.

The following month, on October 22, Ingrid's ship, the MS *Remmaren*, became the eighth casualty among the lejdtrafiken vessels. Captain Hultgren's successor was apparently neither as skillful nor as lucky as he. Transiting from Buenos Aires to Gothenburg with a cargo of linseed meal, hides and wool, the ship struck a minefield in the North Sea. After two large explosions, she sank quickly, but not before all forty-two aboard managed to escape in four lifeboats. It is not clear whether Ingrid was even aware of this until after the war had ended.

Despite having registered for the draft, Arne had not been called up, probably because of his fragile health. Another consideration may have been the critical role he was already playing in the war effort through the planning and routing of convoys across the Atlantic.

Chapter 15

Alice's First Christmas

"A home becomes much richer with a little child!"

By November Arne had almost completely recovered from the troubles with his stomach, although he still had occasional flare-ups. But now he also began to be plagued by lumbago, or lower back pain, walking around with his body bent at what Ingrid described as a forty-five degree angle. This portended what would turn out to be a lifelong problem.

Still, Arne and Ingrid looked forward to their first Christmas with little Alice. In addition to gifts, Arne purchased a variety of Swedish candle holders and other decorations, and Ingrid, mindful of his dietary restrictions, prepared a scaled back smörgåsbord on Christmas Eve. After dinner, they sat in front of their Christmas tree and watched Alice open her presents. Ingrid commented, *"Her eyes were sparkling, reflecting all the candles, and she was so happy. In fact, a home becomes much richer with a little child!"* They got up early Christmas morning, in time to feed Alice before going to a 7 a.m. service as a family.

The following day Ingrid received a long letter from her brother Erik, which had been mailed in September. It was her only greeting from home that Christmas.

On December 30, Arne treated both Ingrid and Anna-Lisa to a lobster dinner in New York, followed by a visit to the planetarium. Ingrid was awed by yet another new experience in what was to become her adopted country. Early on New Year's Eve she wrote,

> "It was the most grandiose and interesting thing I have ever seen. We were in a big room with a spherical roof. An old professor gave an introduction, and then the light faded out. We could see the sparkling stars above our heads, and we had the absolute feeling of being outside in the open air. The starry sky was produced by some strange equipment in a big black box. The position of the stars could be shown at different times, so we also saw the configuration at the time of Christ's birth. One theory is that the three planets Mars, Jupiter and Saturn were so close together that they could look like one big star, the star of Bethlehem. There was also beautiful Christmas music and singing. The only drawback was that we had to look up in the 'sky,' so our necks hurt. Poor Arne, sitting bent forward tried to sit upside down in the chair to be able to see at least something! He is home today, his back worse than ever since last night."

Ingrid's final diary entry was written that evening, and it was full of hope:

> "Now there are only two hours left in 1942. Arne and I are sitting in front of the fire, not a very warming one because the wood is wet. We would have liked to go to church tonight, but it is hard to

get a babysitter on New Year's Eve. And it is okay to welcome the New Year, just the two of us. So many things have happened this last year, both good and bad. But we have more reason to be grateful than to complain. Little Alice has arrived, and she brings us lots of joy. May God help us to be good parents. We don't know what will happen in 1943. Let us hope and pray that there will be peace in the world and that we may see our dear families in Scandinavia in the not too distant future."

CHAPTER 16

The War Years

"I can never eat rabbit today!"

Ingrid and Arne had grown to like Crestwood very much, and they had made a number of good friends among their neighbors. In November 1942, after Arne's recovery, they began to look for a house to buy. One of their criteria was to keep a safe distance from Troublesome Brook! They again turned to their friend Fred Nehring for help. A realtor from his office showed them several properties, but none seemed quite right.

Then in early 1943, Fred steered Arne to a large English Tudor in a beautiful enclave of Crestwood. It had been custom built in 1927 by the developer for his daughter and son-in-law, and seemingly no expense had been spared. The construction cost was said to have been $67,000, an enormous sum at that time. Fred told Arne that the house had gone into foreclosure and that the bank was asking $27,000. Arne told Fred that he couldn't possibly afford that price. "Oh," Fred replied, "it will go for a lot less. Why don't you bid $12,000." With Fred's continued guidance, Arne and Ingrid ultimately purchased the house for $14,000, with a mortgage rate of three percent. They moved into their new home on April 26, 1943, when Ingrid was almost five months pregnant with their second child.

I was born on August 31, and, growing up, that Tudor house was the only home I ever knew. One of my earliest memories is seeing my mother get on her bicycle to go grocery shopping, thereby preserving their limited gasoline ration. The bicycle had a very large basket! My parents would live at 365 Hollywood Avenue for nearly thirty-eight years.

365 Hollywood Avenue as it appeared in the mid 1940s

Meanwhile, Arne's brother Torbjørn was serving with the Allied Forces as a doctor. After stints in Iceland and Scotland, he was transferred to the remote island of Jan Mayen in the Arctic Ocean, about 150 miles north of the Arctic Circle. He was the only doctor throughout a long, dark winter at the small army base there and had to perform some operations for the first time in his life by consulting a book! During his time in Scotland in 1944, one of his colleagues was the Norwegian army doctor, Colonel Leif Øverland, who showed him a picture of his daughter Hjørdis, which had been taken several years earlier when she was just fifteen years old. Torbjørn later was to remember having offered some sort of gratuitous compliment and then thinking nothing more of it.

The War Years

It was only after the war that Ingrid and Arne were to learn how the rest of his family had suffered. The German occupation resulted in food shortages throughout Norway, as the country lost all of its major trading partners from the moment it was occupied. There was a real risk of famine. Many Norwegians started growing their own crops and keeping their own livestock. People raised pigs, rabbits, chickens and other poultry in their houses and yards. Fishing and hunting became more widespread.

Several years before the war, Arne's older brother Ragnar had moved to Sandefjord, a picturesque coastal town about two hours south of Oslo, to take a position with Thor-Dahl, a local shipping company. There he met and fell in love with Johanne Jacobsen. They were married on New Year's Eve in 1938.

In the early stages of the occupation, Sandefjord fared better than the capital Oslo. In a letter to his father in May 1940, a month after the German invasion, Ragnar noted that his town was very quiet, so much so that his company closed its office at two o'clock in the afternoon since they were no longer able to receive any mail or telegrams. A month later a contingent of Germans arrived. To spare its employees from being placed in work camps, the company dispatched some into the surrounding woods to fell trees for firewood and equipped others with fishing tackle so that they could get fish for their families.

Like many of their fellow citizens, Ragnar and Johanne planted a garden from which they harvested tomatoes, onions, lettuce and carrots. They also had several fruit trees, as well as a pig, a number of chickens and a rabbit. On August 2, Johanne gave birth to their first of four daughters and Lydia's and Stefanus' first grandchild. They christened her Inger Marie. Sixteen months later, on Valentine's Day, 1942, she delivered her second child, Berit Johanne.

On November 28, 1943 there was a fire in the Aula, or Great Hall, at the University of Oslo. The material damage was minimal, but the Nazi authorities did not take the incident lightly. Although they immediately suspected communist university students of the incendiarism, the fire was used as a pretext for a general crackdown on students, as had been desired by Reichskommissar Josef Terboven for some time. That evening, Terboven ordered the closing of the university as well as the arrest of all male students. Word of his decision leaked out and warning leaflets were printed and distributed, but many disbelieved it and failed to act. A total of 1,166 students were arrested and rounded up in the ceremony hall. Women were released, but the male students and some faculty were sent to temporary detention camps. One of those students was Arne's youngest brother, Johannes.

More than six hundred of the students were sent on to Germany, where seventeen of them perished in "readjustment" camps. Johannes was first sent to a Nazi detention camp at Stavern, not far from Sandefjord. In early 1944 he was one of just fifteen students transferred to Grini, a facility outside of Oslo originally built as a women's prison. During the occupation it had been first used by the Nazi regime as a detention site before being converted in June 1941 into perhaps Norway's most infamous concentration camp. It became the site of numerous interrogations and torture at the hands of the Gestapo, as well as an unknown number of executions.

Once at Grini, Johannes was denied any contact with his family. Packages of food from Ragnar and letters from other relatives were returned unopened to the sender. In September 1944, Ragnar imposed on a colleague, who served as his firm's liaison with the Gestapo headquarters in Oslo, to present a letter he had written. In it he asked permission for his widowed mother to visit her son. The obersturmbannführer promised to take care of the letter and give Ragnar's colleague a prompt reply. Two weeks later he called to say that he could not help. But in October a letter was delivered to the family home at Huitfeldtsgate 12. It came from the Gestapo headquarters at Victoria Terrasse in Oslo and requested a meeting. Lydia went, accompanied by her son Birger, and somehow managed to obtain permission to see Johannes....alone. She remarked that he looked well, although he was very thin. We do not know what she might have said to his German captors, but after her visit Johannes received permission to write.

One of Johannes' fellow prisoners at Grini was a young woman who would later become his sister-in-law. Twenty-two-year-old Rønnaug Bay was arrested on Karl Johans Gate, a major thoroughfare in downtown Oslo, for turning her back on a company of German soldiers that was marching past. She had arrived by train from the country and was carrying a backpack full of berries and other foodstuffs for some of her relatives, since it was difficult to obtain such goods in the city. Her father was allowed to come to the police station to retrieve the food, but Rønnaug was imprisoned for seven months, from August 16, 1943 until March 16, 1944. The charge: hostile behavior toward Germans. She remembered her prison number, 12423, for the rest of her life.

Lydia continued to shepherd her family in Oslo through the end of the war. She even managed to send some food to Sandefjord to help fatten the family pig in preparation for Christmas in 1944. Ragnar responded by sending her part of the butchered pig, along with some fish. While the family was in church during Christmas, a sortie of six Allied bombers tried to take out Victoria Terrasse, but they missed, succeeding only in leveling a nearby building and shattering countless window panes. The damage at Huitfeldsgate 12 was limited to a few broken glasses. Over the next few months Sandefjord also became the target of frequent bombings, often sending Ragnar, Johanne and their young daughters running for cover. It was the Nazis' last gasp.

On May 8, a joyful Ragnar wrote his mother:

"On this first day of freedom when the newspaper proclaims 'Peace in Europe' I have to write since it is not possible to call. I am very excited to learn whether Johannes has been freed from Grini. He probably is, I hope. I sent a telegram this evening: 'Please call for parcel addressed to Johannes, Vestbanen, Oslo. Hilsen, Ragnar.' It is unbelievable that we finally have peace in Norway after five years of war. It is the end of a nightmare. I am sitting here hearing the news from Sweden. We got our radio back today. This afternoon our two churches here were filled with people in services of thanksgiving. There are more flags flying in town than on May 17! As of this morning we have telegraph connections with Sweden. Have you sent a message to Arne's family? Now I hope that we and the Norwegian people will be grateful that the war is over at last and will celebrate the peace in a worthy way."

After her release from Grini, Rønnaug resumed activity with the Christian Student Association. This group often worshiped in the Nordmarka Chapel, a wooden structure in a forest north of Oslo. It had been built in 1933 by students who wanted to provide a place of worship for young people who went skiing during the winter months. Rønnaug, who was very musical, played its rather antiquated organ during worship. The instrument required the assistance of a volunteer who treaded bellows to provide air while it was being played. One young man came to do this more and more frequently, and he soon was courting the organist. His name: Oddvar Pettersen, Johannes' older brother. He and Rønnaug were married the following year, after the liberation of Norway, on All Saints Day, November 1, 1945.

As it turned out, Johannes did not leave Grini until January 10, 1946. Prisoners of ten to twelve different nationalities were finally sent home to their respective countries. Of these, the Russians received the worst welcome. Unbeknownst to President Roosevelt and Prime Minister Churchill, Stalin had declared that, by surrendering to the Germans, they had betrayed their country. They were arrested and sent to Siberia.

****

One of Arne's siblings was spared the German occupation. On November 30, 1929, his older sister

Lydia Marie went to bed with a headache and fever. Over the next several weeks she was seen by several doctors and underwent a number of tests, all inconclusive. The presumption was that she had a severe case of influenza, and she was told to rest as much as possible. But her condition worsened. On Friday, January 3, she was admitted to Ullevål, the Oslo University Hospital, where she was diagnosed with pyaemia, a bacterial infection of the blood. With antibiotics not yet discovered, her disease was terminal. She breathed her last on Saturday, January 11, 1930, Arne's and Johannes' birthday. She was just twenty years old.

****

As the Swedish government managed to maintain the country's official neutrality during the war, their citizenry was spared many of the privations inflicted on their neighbor to the west. Nevertheless, life certainly changed. Diplomats maintained a delicate balancing act, managing concessions on each side. During the German invasion of Russia, Sweden allowed the Wehrmacht to use its railways to transport troops and weaponry from Norway to Finland. German soldiers travelling on leave from Norway to Germany were allowed passage through Sweden, and the country sold iron ore to Germany throughout the war. However, Swedish authorities also tapped the telegraph lines crossing their country from Norway to Germany and shared valuable military intelligence with the Allies. They also helped train Danish and Norwegian refugee soldiers for the liberation of their home countries and provided sanctuary for Jewish refugees from all over the region.

Although she was just six years old at the time, my cousin Linnéa still remembers the feeling of depression that suddenly changed the atmosphere in her home in Brålanda upon hearing the radio reports of the German occupation of Norway. She recalls that in August 1940 her family experienced military exercises in her neighborhood, with Swedish tanks driving across fields and airplanes flying very low. Similar exercises were apparently being staged throughout Sweden during the war in support of Prime Minister Per Albin Hansson's assertions, "Our preparedness is good." According to Linnéa, "He lied."

The family kitchen was virtually changed into a military cafe, and soldiers freely picked apples from trees in their yard. She had just started going to school and was very scared. Her father (my Uncle Erik) bicycled into town to buy food and had to use rationing coupons. Access to meat was limited to rabbits the family raised in a cage in their garden. She comments, "I can never eat rabbit today!"

As Erik and his family lived close to the railway, they periodically saw the trains carrying German soldiers on leave, a concession that dismayed many Swedes and provoked much criticism of the government. Local press coverage indicated that public opinion was divided. *Göteborgs Stiftstidning*, edited by Ivar Rhedin, was very pro-German, while *Göteborgs Handels och Sjofartstidning*, edited by Torgny Segerstedt, dared to attack Hitler and Goering and their brutality to such an extent that Goering tried to prohibit critical journalism in Swedish papers.

CHAPTER 17

Peace at Last

"I am going to see Jesus today."

As reported in the previous chapter, Oddvar was the first of Arne's five younger brothers to be married after the war. Less than eight months later, on June 22, 1946, Birger was wed to Kari Knutsen.

Torbjørn returned to Norway to conclude his medical studies in Oslo. He reconnected with his former colleague Dr. Leif Øverland and met his daughter Hjørdis, now a lovely young woman, at her father's house in September 1945. They were married the following year, just before Christmas, on December 19, 1946. Six months later, on June 28, 1947, Henry married Else Knutsen. And finally, Johannes, the youngest, was married to Liv Westerby on June 16, 1951.

Neither of Arne's two surviving sisters ever married. Gudrun held a number of clerical positions with different companies in Oslo and, for a number of years, lived in her own apartment at Huitfeldtsgate 12. Astri became a nurse and came to the United States for part of her training before returning to Norway.

Shortly after the war, Lydia's seven youngest children shed the Pettersen surname, as had her three siblings who had moved to the United States forty years earlier. They all adopted the name Elgvin. Ragnar and Arne, who were both already well established in business, opted not to make the change.

Ingrid and Arne were anxious to get back to see their families, but there was no opportunity to do so until the summer of 1946. Also, Arne needed to meet with his business colleagues at Fearnley and Eger's offices in Oslo. He booked passage for his family on the S/S *Stavangerfjord* of the Norwegian-America line, the same ship on which Torbjørn had sailed on his 1940 passage to the United States. In anticipation of an extended visit, Arne also arranged to ship his car. To this day, some of my cousins still remember a large green Buick, the likes of which they had never seen before.

Erik, Ingrid and Alice (ca. 1945)

Built near Liverpool before the end of World War I, *Stavangerfjord* had been requisitioned by the Germans in September 1940 and used as a troop depot ship for the remainder of the war. She was refitted for passenger service in early 1946 and departed on her first sailing from Oslo to New York, via Bergen, on May 31.

I have been unable to determine the exact date of our departure, but my father's passport was stamped in Bergen on August 18. I believe the average trans-Atlantic transit time was around eleven days, so we probably left New York some time in early August. At the time of my third birthday, we were staying in Oslo with my grandmother Lydia. Three days later, we drove across the border into Sweden, and my mother was reunited with her father, her siblings and their families for the first time in more than five years. We stayed in Scandinavia until November, arriving back in New York on the *Stavangerfjord* on November 29, 1946.

Lydia with her first five grandchildren (left to right: Inger, Erik, Alice, Gerd and Berit), in late summer/early fall of 1946.

At some point during our stay, Arne's beautiful Buick had an unfortunate encounter with a truck while negotiating a narrow mountain road. Rather than ship the damaged car back to the U.S., he left it with his brother Henry. According to family lore, in disposing of the car Henry realized almost enough money to cover the purchase of a house, where his son, my cousin Gunnar Elgvin, and his family live to this day.

In the summer of 1947, Torbjørn returned to New York with Hjørdis to complete his medical residency at Bellevue Hospital in New York. Ingrid and Arne welcomed them into their home, where they were to stay for a year. Ingrid was well into her third trimester with her third child, and she recalled that on the day of their arrival it was incredibly hot and humid. Hjørdis' reaction was similar to what Ingrid's had been upon her arrival in Brooklyn six years earlier. She tried to assure Hjørdis that the weather would get cooler and told her that they often got snow in the winter. Hjørdis replied that she would gladly shovel any snow that fell. Four months later, the Great Blizzard of 1947 began on Christmas morning. By the time it ended the following day, Crestwood had been blanketed with three feet of snow. Arne took home movies to record Hjørdis' futile attempt to fulfill her promise before he and Torbjørn picked up shovels and assisted.

On September 28, Ingrid gave birth to a second daughter, who was christened Margaret Christina. She was to have three more children: Stephen Daniel, born on May 1, 1951; Barbara Elizabeth, born on October 8, 1953, who was called by her middle name; and Astrid Catharina, born during a major snowstorm on February 16, 1958.

After our return from Scandinavia, Mom realized that Crestwood was now home. She became a naturalized American citizen in 1949 and soon spoke English fluently with virtually no accent. She told me she realized that she had become an American when she found herself thinking in English!

That same year, Lydia traveled to America aboard the *Stavangerfjord*, as two of her sons had done before her, returning to Oslo several months later.

She continued to preside as the beloved matriarch of her growing family and always remembered the birthdays of every one of her twenty-eight grandchildren. On March 27, 1976, at the age of ninety-four, she told her daughter Astri, "I am going to see Jesus today."

Daniel Sillén continued to serve his parish in Gesäter until March 29, 1950, when he went home to be with his Lord and his beloved Alice. They are both buried in the church cemetery, sharing a plot with their infant son Ivar.

CHAPTER 18

Early Memories

Train up a child in the way he should go; Even when he is old, he will not depart from it. Proverbs 22:6

During our formative years, our parents instilled the habit of regular attendance at both Sunday School and church, and Dad regularly led evening devotions for the family around the dinner table. As soon as we were able, we children took turns in reading the appointed Bible verses that went with the lesson.

Before seatbelts! Alice, Erik and Margaret in the family's 1950 Buick station wagon, ca. 1950-51 (Note: It is parked!)

Mom gave all of us an appreciation for music. She had a beautiful soprano voice and sang in the church choir. I also have fond memories of the way she ended each day with me when I was very young and ready to go to bed. She would read a selection from the *Bible Story Book* by Elsie Egermeier, then listen to me say my prayers before she tucked me in for the night.

The Pettersen family, ca. 1954. Left to right: Margaret, Alice, Elizabeth, Ingrid, Stephen, Arne and Erik.

We celebrated Christmas with what we thought was the best blend of Scandinavian and American traditions. We children had individual Advent calendars, opening up a little window each day in our countdown to Christmas. Mom made an annual pilgrimage to a Scandinavian delicatessen in Hartsdale, about four miles away, to stock up on delicacies for her smörgåsbord. We sang Christmas carols going both there and back. We all participated in putting up decorations in the house, including a manger scene with freshly cut evergreen branches behind it. We always had a fresh cut tree but didn't put it up and decorate it until the 23rd of December. On the morning of Christmas Eve, we all placed our presents under the tree, many with rhymes of varying quality to give a clue as to the contents.

The family in 1958, left to right: Alice, Margaret, Arne, Astrid, Elizabeth, Ingrid, Stephen and Erik.

The smörgåsbord would be served around four o'clock, and we were each allowed to choose and open one present before leaving for the Christmas Eve service at church. This served to heighten our anticipation of the rest of our gifts. Shortly after our return home, Santa Claus would appear on the terrace outside of our living room, knocking loudly on the windows. When I was very young, I have to confess that I was absolutely terrified of him. It was only after finding a large mail bag in our basement and then associating Santa's presence with my father's absence that my fears were allayed.

Epilogue

Rejoice in the Lord always!
Phil. 4:4

Ingrid and Arne lived in Crestwood until January 1981, around the time of Arne's seventieth birthday, when they downsized and moved about eighty miles north to the historic town of Rhinebeck, New York. They left a house filled with many memories. Most were happy ones, but some were tragic. With their emphasis on education, all of their children had earned college degrees and five would go on to earn advanced degrees as well. All had married, and they had produced six grandchildren.

But the preceding years had not been easy. They were presaged by the passing in 1961 of Sir Thomas Fearnley, the man who had hand-picked Arne to establish and expand his company's operations in the United States twenty-four years earlier. In 1964, Arne was forced out of Fearnley and Eger by new management in Oslo. Although only fifty-three at the time, he had been with the firm for thirty-seven years and had run the New York office for most of his twenty-seven years in the United States. He struck out on his own, but with at best mixed results.

Ingrid went back to school, successfully passed all of the requisite examinations and became a registered nurse in 1968. For the next thirteen years she worked the night shift at a home for the aged.

Early in the morning of December 23, 1978, while driving from their home in upstate New York to Crestwood in their compact Chevrolet Vega for Christmas, Elizabeth and her husband Fred Johnson were hit head-on by a drunk driver in a Corvette. Fred sustained a number of lacerations but Elizabeth's injuries proved fatal. She had to be pried free from the wreckage and died several hours later in a hospital in Goshen, New York. She was only twenty-five, and her untimely passing left some deep scars.

Toward the end of 1984, Arne suffered a heart attack but recovered after a brief hospitalization. Just a few months later, in early 1985, Ingrid was diagnosed with breast cancer and underwent a radical mastectomy. True to form, she used her experience as a platform to visit and encourage other women dealing with and recovering from the same surgery. About five years later, as her sight began to fail, she was diagnosed with macular degeneration and soon had to give up driving, greatly curtailing her many volunteer activities.

Ingrid went home to be with her Lord on April 8, 1995, which happened to be her father's birthday. It was just one day shy of the fifty-fifth anniversary of receiving Arne's letter proposing to her. Arne remained in their home in Rheinbeck until his passing in September 1999.

Ingrid and Arne had planned their funeral services years earlier, complete with Scripture readings and hymns. Ingrid's instructions were especially clear: It was to be a time for celebration, not mourning. Their tombstone is inscribed with the beginning of her favorite verse, Philippians 4:4 – "Rejoice in the Lord always!"

ACKNOWLEDGMENTS

My primary source for this narrative was my mother, who gave me a recording of her recollections from her childhood and youth. After her passing in 1995, I discovered her diaries from the early months of my parents' marriage. These were translated into English for me by my dear late cousin Stig Törnqvist of Rälta, Sweden.

My father's efforts in tracing the family's genealogy laid the groundwork for several of my other cousins, who have continued to keep abreast of and to document later generations. On my father's side in Norway, I gratefully acknowledge the assistance of my dear cousins Odd Helge Elgvin and Rev. Torleif Elgvin of Oslo, Ragne Moe of Sandefjord and Inger Marie Bach-Evensen of Kristiansand; and Svein Elgvin, the son of my late cousin Tron, of Arendal. On my mother's side in Sweden, in addition to Stig, my cousins Carl-Erik Törnqvist of Kinna, Karin Lindqvist of Torsby and Linnéa Melander of Ängelholm have provided patient answers to my repeated inquiries. Carl-Erik even sent a DVD of home movies made by my Swedish family in 1937.

After hearing of my intent to write this story when we reconnected at a reunion of our Norwegian family in the summer of 2009, Ragne told me of a letter which my mother had written her parents shortly after her honeymoon. She subsequently provided me with an English translation, which appears on pages 75 through 81.

Bernice Hoveland Hardy (nee Ragnvald), a first cousin of my father and now ninety-five years young, hosted me for a wonderful day in her home in Bethesda, Maryland on January 11, 2012, which, had he lived, would have been my father's 101st birthday. She supplied me with family stories and photographs and clarified my understanding of our family tree. After my visit she continued to be my faithful e-mail partner, patiently responding to my questions as they came up. A more distant relative, Alf Brorson, was gracious enough to provide me with a copy of his book, *Sillénska Anfäder – tolv präster i Värmland och på Dal (Sillén Family Ancestors – Twelve Priests in Värmland and Dal)*, which chronicles the careers of the clergy in my mother's family, including those of my grandfather and two uncles.

My brother Stephen, of Wynantskill, New York, and my sister Alice Meyer of Silver Spring, Maryland, responded to multiple requests, retrieving and sending a number of choice photographs. As the unofficial family archivist, Stephen was also a valuable sounding board throughout this project, unearthing additional precious resources of which I was unaware. These included my parents' guest book and my father's original passport, which documents his travels from his emigration to the United States in 1937 up to 1950, when he was naturalized as an American citizen.

I also owe a debt of gratitude to my dear friend and fellow author, Cyndy Crowner, who volunteered to review my manuscript and suggested a number of helpful changes.

And, finally, I would be remiss if I were not to acknowledge and thank my daughter Kristen Pettersen

Acknowledgments

Morgan of Stafford, Virginia. She had a special bond with her "Farmor" and evinced interest in this endeavor from the start. She graciously reviewed my first draft, offered a number of constructive suggestions and agreed to write the foreword.

One of the true blessings of this project was the opportunity to collaborate with Scandinavian relatives whom I see all too infrequently. I should specifically mention my cousin Inger, whom I cannot recall having seen since my first visit to Norway in 1946. (See the picture on page 143.) As soon as we reconnected, she proved to be the exceptional family historian that Bernice told me she was. I owe much to her for the many pictures and descriptions she provided, as well as her recollections of the war years in Norway. On one day in April, during which we exchanged multiple e-mails, she wrote, "I think our fathers, Ragnar and Arne, would have appreciated our contact," to which I could only respond, "I think so, too!"

NOTES

Chapter 1 – The Beginning

1. Magnus's son Haakon VI and his infant son Olav IV were Norway's last native kings until Harald V ascended to the throne in 1991.

Chapter 2 -- The Silléns – A Family of Clergy

2. The stroke over the "e" in Sillén is very important. Without it, sillen means herring!

Chapter 6 -- "Iron Brain"

3. The *Ferncliff* was built in Hamburg, Germany in 1924 by Deutsche Werft AG and displaced 4,333 gross tons. It became an essential unit in the convoys which Arne was to arrange between North America and Great Britain during World War II. This was interrupted by its use as a military transport for the Torch operations (the invasion of North Africa) in November of 1942.

4. Arne's passport shows a stamp by "Passkontroll" in Norway on 10/26/1938, a stay in Göteborg from 11/5-8/1938, and a stop in London on 11/10/1938 ("Landed as Transmigrant under Bond"). We have no record of his having seen Ingrid while he was in Göteborg. His passport kept getting renewed by the Consulate General of Norway in New York until he was granted naturalized citizenship on 7/20/1950.

Chapter 7 – Ingrid's Post-Adolescence

5. Vidkun Quisling was a notorious Norwegian politician who assisted Nazi Germany as it conquered his own country so that he could rule the

collaborationist government himself. Thanks to the British press, his surname became synonymous with "traitor."

Chapter 8 – American Bride

6. During the early part of the war, Sweden found another route to ship west via the port town of Petsamo (now Petjenga) in northernmost Finland on the Arctic Ocean. This traffic developed rapidly over the summer of 1940 and was allowed by Britain, who were thereby able to obtain critical Swedish ball bearing parts. By midsummer 1941, however, the port was completely shut down, and Finland ultimately lost all of its territory on the Arctic Ocean to the Russians.

7. The Battle of the Denmark Strait, a major naval engagement between the British Royal Navy and the German Kriegsmarine, and involving the famed battlecruiser HMS *Hood* and the German battleship *Bismarck*, was fought on May 24, 1941, during the early days of my mother's voyage.

8. In addition to the misspellings in this paragraph, the *Herald Tribune* reporter also confused the final destinations of the eminent professors. Roman Osipovich Jakobson was to become one of the most influential linguists of the twentieth century. Born in Moscow in 1896 and of Jewish extraction, he escaped from Prague at the beginning of the war, moving successively to Denmark, Norway and, finally, to Sweden. When Swedish colleagues began to fear a possible German occupation, he managed to book passage on the *Remmaren*. It was he who went to Harvard, teaching there until his retirement, and then continuing as a professor emeritus at M.I.T until his death in 1982. Ernst Cassirer, also from a Jewish family, was chair of the philosophy department at

Notes

the University of Hamburg until 1933, when the Nazis came to power. He fled to Oxford in England and then to Gothenburg University. After arriving in New York, his first destination was Yale University. He later moved to Columbia University, where he taught until his death at the age of seventy on April 13, 1945.

9. Given the circumstances, this was a wedding in which the groom made up the guest list. It appears that Ingrid's contribution was limited to her recent friend – and bridesmaid! – Anna-Lisa Montheli. A New York newspaper article listed the following attendees at the reception: Dr. and Mrs. Walter A. Maier, Rev. and Mrs. Paul H Scaer, Mr. and Mrs. C.B. Bendixen, Captain Oddvar Blindheim, Mr. Birger Gran, Rev. Leif Gulbrandsen, Mr. Bjørn Lie, Miss Anna-Lisa Montheli, Mr. and Mrs. Fred. W. Nehring, Mr. and Mrs. Charles Nordstrøm, Miss May Peterson, Mr. and Mrs. Arthur Nordstrøm, Captain Anker Pettersen, Miss Ruth Ragnvald [Aunt Ruth], Mr. Torbjørn Pettersen [Arne's younger brother], Mr. Fritz Rustad, Mr. and Mrs. R-A. Smith, Mr. Johannes Wallin, Mr. John Wallin, Miss Florence Zimmermann, Mr. and Mrs. Gustav Zimmermann. Many of the attendees were to play a prominent role in the lives of the newlyweds.

Chapter 10 – The Early War Years

10. Santa Lucia's (Saint Lucy's) Day is a Church feast day observed on the 13th of December and is one of the few saint days observed in Scandinavia.

Chapter 11 – First Christmas in America

11. Glögg is a sweet, high-octane, mulled wine, made with a variety of spices and a mixture of claret (red wine), port, and brandy. Because it is served warm,

it is especially popular around Christmas in Sweden. It has been described as the perfect cold-weather drink, warming the body and soul from the inside out. In Arne's recipe the alcohol content was sufficient to make the surface flammable, and he would light it before bringing the serving bowl to his guests.

Chapter 12 – A New Year

12. During World War II the Army Transport Service operated a total of twenty-four hospital ships which were manned by "civilian" crews, employees of the Army Transport Service. The embarked medical staff were Army personnel. The hospital ships were operated under the provisions of the Hague Convention X of 1907, which specified identifying markings. These proved inadequate, so large illuminated red crosses on deck were added for aerial visibility at night. Hospital ships were allowed to carry medical supplies as cargo for the battlefield. Most of the hospital ships were former passenger liners/troopships which were disarmed, repainted, and rearranged for hospital use. The *St. Olaf* could accommodate up to 586 patients and made its maiden voyage to the United Kingdom in July 1944.